THE WOLVERHAMPTON TRAGEDY

Frontispiece: Edward Lawrence (1867–1912).

THE WOLVERHAMPTON TRAGEDY

Death and the 'Respectable' Mr Lawrence

JOHN BENSON

The Wolverhampton Tragedy: Death and the 'Respectable' Mr Lawrence

Copyright © John Benson, 2009

First edition

Published by Carnegie Publishing Ltd
Carnegie House,
Chatsworth Road,
Lancaster, LA1 4SL
www.carnegiepublishing.com

ISBN 978-1-85936-195-5

Typeset by Carnegie Book Production
Printed and bound in the UK by Cromwell Press Group, Trowbridge

Contents

Acknowledgements

I am pleased to take this opportunity to thank those who have helped me in the writing of this book. I am grateful for the financial support of the British Academy and the Scouloudi Foundation, for the publicity my research has received from the *Express and Star*, Smooth Radio and BBC Radio Shropshire, and for the opportunity to present earlier versions of some of my arguments at De Montfort University and the University of Wolverhampton.

I am grateful, too, for the help that I have received not only from friends, colleagues and ex-colleagues but also from a large number of people whom I have never had the opportunity to meet. Adriana Feld and Carol Volante provided valuable research assistance. Peter Ackers, Tom Almond, Owen Ashton, John Buckley, Mike Dennis, Nicholas Birch, Andrew MacLennan, Bill Piggins, Dilwyn Porter, Tim Sheldon, Linda Townsend, Laura Ugolini and Malcolm Wanklyn offered interest and encouragement at crucial times. Adrian Allen, Bev Baker, Rosemary Boyns, Roger Burt, Diane Clements, Nancy Cox, Philip Daw, Martin Elkes, Pam Eves, Roger Fanner, Michael Frost, Mrs Green, Steven Hadley, Paul Henderson, Spenser Jones, Emma Kilvert, Roger Leese, Mark Lees, Brendan McDonagh, Margaret Ponsonby, Lucy Powell, Frank Sharman, Gareth Shaw, Colin Warwick and Harvey Woolf all supplied me with ideas, insights and information.

However, my greatest debts are to Mike Huggins, Laura Ugolini and Carol Volante, each of whom took time from their own work to comment most helpfully on an earlier version of the book. Laura Ugolini, in particular, made a whole series of suggestions, almost all of which I initially rejected – and almost all of which I have tried subsequently to incorporate into the text.

John Benson
September 2008

1

'A terrible tragedy'[1]

Edward Lawrence packed more into his forty-five years than most people living twice as long. Born in Liverpool in 1867, there was little in his childhood and early life to set him apart. Brought up in Wolverhampton in an upwardly mobile, middle-class family, he went to private school, qualified as a veterinary surgeon, set up in practice, and spent two years in South America before returning to his home town in the early 1890s to work in the family drinks business. He married a local woman, Margaret Groom, had seven children, and took over the running of the family business following the deaths of his father and younger brother at the turn of the century.

Thereafter, however, Edward's seemingly secure and respectable life unravelled with remarkable rapidity. Between 1905 and 1910, his drinking escalated, he attacked a policeman, and he assaulted his wife. He was sued by a lover and divorced by his wife. He shot another lover, Ruth Hadley, and was tried and acquitted of her murder. He was declared bankrupt, and pursued through the courts by his estranged wife. He spent the final few years of his life in Kidderminster, where he lived with yet another lover, and made a series of court appearances, 'arising out of domestic infelicities and tradesmen's claims'.[2] He died, almost certainly as a result of his excessive drinking, in the summer of 1912.

It was Edward's shooting of his lover, Ruth Hadley, in December 1908, and his subsequent arrest, prosecution and trial for murder that brought his character, attitudes and behaviour to the attention of his contemporaries, not just in Wolverhampton but, to a lesser extent, across the country as a whole. It was a humbling and humiliating experience, made worse by the fact that his defence team, led by the celebrated barrister Edward Marshall Hall, decided that there was no option but to sacrifice their client's reputation in order to try to save his life. Whatever the costs to Edward's feelings, and whatever its impact upon his life following the trial, the strategy worked. He was acquitted, and walked from the court a free man. When the jury had delivered its verdict, the judge, Mr Justice Jelf, gave Edward what one local paper described as 'some good advice as to his future life'.[3]

> Before I discharge you, I want to add a few words of advice to those which your brilliant counsel have already, I have no doubt, given to you. You have had a most terrible lesson. You have been mixed up with a terrible tragedy. You have had now, in the time you have been in prison an opportunity of seeing what is the difference between a man with the use of his senses and his feelings which God had given him unprepared for that horrible fiend of drink; and you have also had the opportunity of seeing how your wife has been so grievously wronged some time ago, and who yet has been ready to forgive you. And I think it is possible that if you turn over a new leaf you may yet have a happy time with your lawful wife and children, and that you may be forgiven by God for your past life. I say this for your family's sake, because I think, having acted this awful experience, you must feel how much of all that has happened has been due to your own habits and immorality; and I hope that what I have said before will bear fruit in your after life. 'Thank you, my Lord', replied Lawrence, standing erect in the dock.[4]

The trial was over, but the case of Rex *v*. Lawrence[5] raises a whole series of questions. Who was Edward Lawrence? Who was Ruth Hadley? How did they meet, and how did she come to die? Was Ruth's death an accident? Or was it manslaughter, or murder? If it was murder, did Lawrence get away with it, as the judge seemed to imply, thanks largely to the efforts of his 'brilliant counsel'? Once he was acquitted, did he 'turn over a new leaf'? Did he go on to 'have a happy time' with his wife and children, as Justice Jelf hoped? Did Lawrence's experience of arrest, imprisonment, trial and acquittal 'bear fruit' – whatever that might mean – in the years that lay ahead of him until his death in 1912? What, if anything, does Edward Lawrence's shooting of Ruth Hadley tell us about the late Victorian and Edwardian world in which they lived?

The typical and the untypical

Such questions, of course, are a good deal easier to ask than they are to answer. Nevertheless, it is tempting to persuade oneself that with hindsight one can understand people's behaviour, distinguish the significant from the insignificant, disentangle the most labyrinthine of circumstances, and reconstruct even the most convoluted sequence of cause and effect. But the very greatest caution is called for. Time and distance afford great opportunities, it is true, but they also pose considerable dangers.

When I set out to undertake this study, I was no means certain that I would be able to uncover the sources required for it to be completed anything like satisfactorily. It was one thing to acquire material on the trial itself, and to obtain certain basic information concerning the key protagonists. But would it be possible to uncover evidence of the range and richness required to think realistically of tackling the sorts of questions in which I was interested?

In the event, it proved possible to draw upon the fact that unhappy marriages, failing businesses and deaths in suspicious circumstances tended – and tend – to leave fuller and more revealing records than happy marriages, successful businesses and deaths from natural causes. Thus, when Edward Lawrence's wife sued him for divorce in 1905, the Probate, Divorce and Admiralty Division of the High Court of Justice compiled a detailed set of court minutes (now in the National Archives).[6] When Lawrence was charged with assaulting one of his mistresses in 1907, the local press took a keen – not to say salacious – interest in the proceedings.[7] When he was arrested, charged and tried for murder in 1908–9, the press – regional and national as well as local – covered the case, and the police compiled a file (also in the National Archives) on his 'antecedents', which contained, *inter alia*, a medical report, police testimony and a number of witness statements.[8] When he was declared bankrupt in 1910, the local press returned to the fray, providing yet more evidence of what they saw as his moral and financial failings.[9] Then, when Edward Lawrence moved to Kidderminster during the final few years of his life, the press there reported with some relish the misadventures in which he continued to get himself involved.[10]

The problem is, of course, that these sources all emanate from the final few years of Lawrence's life, and that they all provide a consistent – and therefore seemingly convincing – view of his character and behaviour. The challenge facing the historian therefore is to try to isolate oneself from this perspective, to do one's best to assess the evidence, whether 'witting' or 'unwitting', with as much sensitivity and intelligence as one can muster.[11]

This is not easy. Indeed, in many respects, this is the most difficult book that I have ever written. In the past, I have been happy enough to analyse, to my own satisfaction at least, any number of major economic and social developments. I have explained why, for instance, hundreds of thousands of nineteenth-century coal miners joined friendly societies and trade unions,[12] and why it was that millions upon millions of twentieth-century women decided to increase their spending on cosmetics and consumer durables.[13] But in writing this book, I have often found it hard to tackle what seem on the face of it, to be much simpler and more straightforward questions. It has been a salutary reminder of the limitations not only of my own abilities, but of the biographical approach, and perhaps indeed of the entire historical enterprise.

Accident, manslaughter or murder?

It is possible to read this book in a number of ways. It can be read, most obviously, as a 'who-done-it'. Did Edward Lawrence kill Ruth Hadley? If he did, was it an accident, manslaughter or murder? These, of course, are complex questions. It is not always easy to uncover the cause even of contemporary deaths. How much more difficult it is to get to the truth of the matter when the investigation is carried out – extremely – retrospectively. The task here is to decide what happened behind closed doors, between two people, one of whom died within a couple of hours, the other of whom was scarcely a disinterested witness – and both of whom have now been dead for a century.

The question of Edward Lawrence's guilt is by no means as prurient and parochial as it may appear. In fact, it is an issue that serves several other purposes. It can be used, most obviously, to try to understand a man who, though virtually unknown to posterity, led a life that was, by turn, mundane and remarkable, provincial and cosmopolitan, manly and shameful, respectable and disreputable. More interesting still, the question of Lawrence's character and guilt can be used to throw light on a number of issues that are central to a broader understanding of the late nineteenth- and early twentieth-century England in which he lived. The untypical, it is believed, really can be used to elucidate the typical.[14]

If we can decide – beyond reasonable doubt – how Ruth Hadley died, and whether or not Edward Lawrence was rightly acquitted, we should be in a better position to assess, for instance, the nature and efficiency of policing in Edwardian England. Was this a time when a class-based political, legal and law enforcement system discriminated shamelessly in favour of the well off and the well connected? Or was it a time, as many now seem to believe, when a long-lost combination of the 'bobby on the beat' and a judiciary unrestrained by political correctness and external interference ensured that the guilty were punished, the innocent were freed – and justice was done?

Moreover, if we can decide what it was that set Edward Lawrence apart, we should be able to gain a better understanding of other economic, social and cultural forces in operation at the time. Why was it Edward, rather than the millions of his contemporaries, who shot a mistress, found himself charged with murder, forced to hear details of his personal affairs paraded in public, and obliged to listen to a judge's advice as to how best to turn his life around? In attempting to explain how it was that Lawrence came to find himself in this wholly exceptional situation, we will look for clues, as far as we are able, in his upbringing and education, in his married life, in his business career – and in the nature of contemporary society.

It is believed therefore that this book can be read most helpfully as a study of social, cultural and economic relationships in late Victorian and Edwardian England. Edward Lawrence's life, and his shooting of Ruth Hadley, opens a window through which we can explore aspects of English provincial life that most often remain shrouded from view. It offers us glimpses – and more than glimpses – of an unhappy marriage, extramarital affairs and bitter divorce proceedings. Edward Lawrence's life affords us fresh insights into middle-class education, middle-class career choices, working-class solidarities, the power of the press, the emergence of new professions, and the workings of businesses both successful and unsuccessful. It forces us to think hard about gender and class relationships and, about the power, fragility and resilience of middle-class respectability.

Gender

Gender, it goes almost without saying, is of vital importance when seeking to understand personal relationships – indeed almost all aspects of late nineteenth- and early twentieth-century middle-class life. But there have been significant changes in the ways in which historians view Victorian and Edwardian families. It used to be thought that middle-class husbands such as Edward exercised more-or-less unchallenged control over their wives and children.[15] But this belief in an omnipotent paterfamilias has come under serious challenge over recent decades. Female historians, in particular, set out to uncover the achievements of women who succeeded in what was overwhelmingly a man's world.[16] They began to examine women's struggles against male prejudice and oppression;[17] they began to use concepts such as gender and class, culture and domesticity, masculinity and femininity, patriarchy, matriarchy and separate spheres as tools to explain, as well as to describe, men's and women's relationships with one another.[18]

The historical profession, they argued, needed to abandon its old, gender-based stereotypes.[19] And abandon them it did, with scholars, both male and female, developing, in time, a new consensus to take their place. During the nineteenth century, claims John Tosh, there emerged 'an entrepreneurial, individualistic masculinity, organised around a punishing work ethic, a compensating validation of the home, and a restraint on physical aggression.'[20] It was the duty of the middle-class husband to be a judicious and understanding provider – the duty of the middle-class wife to manage the household and to look after the children.[21] Indeed, it has been suggested that during the second half of the century, the widening of educational and employment opportunities, the liberalisation of the divorce laws and the decline in the birth rate both reflected and encouraged the emergence of more companionable marriages. Such developments, it has also been suggested, combined to encourage – and allow – more wives than one would suppose to challenge what they regarded as their husbands' unreasonable authority.[22]

Edward Lawrence's marriage to his wife, Margaret, provides intriguing insights into these, and related, issues.[23] It will be seen that, on the face of it, their relationship seems rooted in an earlier age, untouched by the liberalising developments supposedly changing middle-class marriage during the second half of the nineteenth century. Nor is it difficult to portray Edward as a chauvinist bully, with Margaret his more or less powerless victim. Edward was older than his wife; he probably got her pregnant before they married; and he went on to father a large family of a type that was becoming increasingly unusual in middle-class circles. And as if to confirm his disreputable, chauvinist credentials, he gambled and drank, he embarked upon a series of extra-marital affairs, he had at least two illegitimate children, he abandoned his family, and he sometimes resorted to violence in his arguments with Margaret.

But Margaret, it will be shown, was by no means the helpless casualty she might appear. Whatever she made of Edward's drinking, gambling and sexual adventures, she was prepared – eventually – to stand up to him. Margaret remonstrated with at least one of Edward's mistresses; she gave evidence against him in court; she removed the children from the family home; she sued him for divorce (at a time when this was exceptionally difficult and unusual); and she pursued him doggedly for the maintenance that he had promised, but failed, to pay her. Margaret, it transpires, was neither the powerless victim that the earlier historiography suggests nor the compliant and/or contented companion that more recent studies might lead one to suppose.

Class

Those interested in Victorian and Edwardian family life can scarcely fail to wonder at the presence, within so many middle-class households, of what sometimes seem like small armies of working-class domestic help. Indeed, for many years the few labour, social and feminist historians who examined this sector of the Victorian and Edwardian economy tended to regard the women who worked in it as the epitome of working-class subservience and powerlessness.[24] It was a view shared by those commenting more broadly on late nineteenth- and early twentieth-century life. This was my view of the subject in 1989:

> Despite the popularity in recent years of autobiographies such as Margaret Powell's *Below Stairs* and of television programmes such as 'Upstairs, Downstairs', the lives of the millions of women and girls who worked in domestic service stay stubbornly hidden from view. Yet enough is known to refute any suggestion that their lives underwent much change, let alone change for the better. Their hours remained long and irregular; their work unmechanised, unpleasant and often very lonely. Their relationships with their employers remained characterised by a curious personal-impersonal quality.[25]

It would be difficult today to take such an unequivocally critical view of domestic service. It has been made clear in recent years that working conditions, hours of work and personal relationships all varied much more than used to be thought.[26] It is not surprising perhaps that, 'the well-do with a large staff found it easier to recruit servants than those keeping one or two domestics only'. After all, they offered their employees higher status, more attractive career prospects and more clearly defined work routines.[27] What does seem surprising is that servants everywhere, it is now emphasised, were by no means powerless in their dealings with their masters and mistresses. They 'had their own methods of revenge against unfair treatment, using familiar weapons such as sulking, mishearing orders, semi-deliberate spoiling of materials, wasting time, "the sullen dumb insolence and petty irritations" bemoaned by employers.'[28]

Once again, Edward Lawrence's life provides an intriguing insight into some of the issues surrounding class – and gender – relationships in late Victorian and Edwardian England.[29] The dealings he had with the servants he employed during the course of his life seem to represent on the face of it another example of male, middle-class power and domination, in this case of a married (later divorced) 'master' exploiting his female staff for his sexual gratification. It will be seen that Edward propositioned at least one of his servants (and installed two of his mistresses as members of his domestic staff). He expected all the women he employed, whatever their relationships with him, not just to clean and to cook and to look after his children, but to do exactly as he demanded.

However, it transpires that Edward's dealings with the women he employed – like the woman he married – were by no means as one-sided as they appear at first sight. No doubt, Edward's servants sulked, spoiled materials, misheard instructions and wasted time as much as those employed by anybody else. But they did not confine themselves to such surreptitious, stereotypically female ways of challenging their master's authority. They drew strength, several of them, from the kinship and neighbourhood ties that remained so marked a feature of many working-class communities. Indeed, they sometimes adopted strategies more usually associated with members of the organised labour movement. Three of them withdrew their labour collectively; one of them appealed for police protection, and when this failed took out a summons against Edward for assault.

Respectability

Then, too, there is respectability which, we have been told time and time again, was of absolutely fundamental importance to the Victorian and Edwardian middle class (and indeed to a surprisingly substantial section of the working class).[30] Respectability, we have been led to believe, was difficult to acquire, and all too easy to lose. Indeed, Geoffrey Best maintained as long ago as 1979 that, 'some hall-marks of respectability were absolutely standard'.

> Respectable people did not get drunk (a test which of itself ruled out great numbers of men and women, most but not all of the lower classes) or behave wildly; they maintained a certain propriety of speech and decorum of bearing; they dressed tidily and kept their houses clean and tidy, inside and out; the men's dress and everyone's demeanour were especially sober and decorous on Sundays. They never did or said anything in the presence of persons of lower classes which might offer encouragement or excuse for ill conduct. That they were 'independent' and law-abiding goes without saying.[31]

The thirty years since have seen, it is true, some limited attempts at conceptual and empirical revisionism. Mike Huggins has led the way, suggesting repeatedly – and in my view correctly – that we should not take respectability for granted: 'whilst respectability may have had ideological power, we need to question critically both the extent to which such beliefs were actually held and some of their impact, and explore the notion and significance of an unrespectable set of middle-class values.'[32]

However, the assaults that Huggins and others have launched upon the concept of middle-class respectability (unlike the attacks upon the belief in the all-powerful Victorian and Edwardian paterfamilias or the virtually powerless Victorian and Edwardian domestic servant) have never really adhered. Thus *The Rise of Respectable Society* was the title that F.M.L. Thompson chose to give to his widely praised 1988 social history of Victorian Britain.[33] 'Respectability was vital, not superficial', concluded Simon Gunn and Rachel Bell in their 2002 examination of the late nineteenth-century middle classes: 'Without respectability you could not get credit, your son might not get the right sort of career opening and your daughter might not be able to marry into a well-to-do family.'[34]

Whatever view one takes of the resilient orthodoxy of respectability, its relevance to this book is obvious.[35] We shall see that although Edward Lawrence was brought up respectably, it was a respectability that was under constant threat. It was not just that the Lawrence family depended upon the drink trade. Edward became ensnared in sexual scandal. He was charged with assault, divorced by his wife, arrested for murder, declared bankrupt, dragged through the courts and, as we shall see, came to believe that he was being hounded by the local police. Astonishingly, however, Edward did not, it seems, suffer the overwhelming social opprobrium one would have thought absolutely inevitable. We shall see that, despite all that he had done, despite all that had happened to him, he continued to be afforded some, at least, of the respect that was routinely paid to the respectable middle class in Victorian and Edwardian England.

Scandal, murder and social relationships

Accordingly, this book has two central aims. The first is to acquaint modern readers with Edward Lawrence: who he was, what he did, and what happened to him during the course of a short, but fascinatingly varied life. The second is to use Edward Lawrence's life to consider some of those issues of gender, class and respectability that are of central concern to those interested in the late nineteenth and early twentieth centuries. It is hoped therefore that the book will appeal not just to those interested in scandal, in murder or in the West Midlands, but to all those concerned to learn more about social relationships in late Victorian and Edwardian provincial England.

PART I

RESPECTABILITY

2

'Family history and antecedents'[1]

E DWARD LAWRENCE was born in Liverpool in 1867. It was a time that now seems at once impossibly distant yet recognisably modern. Queen Victoria was on the throne, and Disraeli was prime minister. It was the year that Karl Marx published the first volume of *Das Kapital*, and Joseph Lister reported that carbolic acid could be used to practise antiseptic surgery. It was the year after Alfred Nobel invented dynamite, the year before compulsory church rates were abolished in England and Wales. It was the year that the Second Great Reform Act extended the franchise for the first time to large numbers of working-class men in the country's burgeoning towns and cities.[2]

'In a large way of business'[3]

There was little in Edward Lawrence's childhood and adolescence to set him apart. Indeed his upbringing appeared to represent, on the face of it, almost a textbook example of what it was like to grow up in an upwardly mobile, late Victorian middle-class, provincial family. His father, Joseph, began his working life as a farm servant, probably lived in Liverpool, moved to Wolverhampton, established a successful drink business, did well for himself and, when he was older, went into local politics and became a director of Wolverhampton Wanderers football club. Edward's parents had seven children in quick succession, his mother, Sarah, staying at home to look after them in conventional middle-class fashion. The Lawrences provided a textbook example, too, of the way in which premature death threatened so often to undermine the stability of nineteenth-century family life. One of Edward's siblings died in childhood, and the remaining children lost their mother – and Joseph his wife – while Edward was still in his teens.

Joseph's and Sarah Lawrence's decision to move to Wolverhampton was one small part of the large-scale urban migration that became associated so

Edward Lawrence's father, Joseph Lawrence (1835–1901), built up a thriving
drinks business, was elected a Conservative town councillor and became a
director of Wolverhampton Wanderers football club.

closely with late eighteenth- and nineteenth-century industrial expansion.
Wolverhampton, it is true, might not seem an obvious destination. Then,
as now, it suffered from a reputation for unprepossessing provincialism:[4] the
year before Edward was born, *Punch* reacted with what has been described
as 'abusive astonishment' when it learned that Queen Victoria had decided

to visit the town on one of her first public appearances following the death of her beloved Albert.[5]

But Wolverhampton was a sensible enough choice for an aspiring publican. One of the country's rapidly growing industrial towns, it was home by 1871 to nearly 70,000 people (as well as over 200 inns, taverns and beerhouses).[6] The town, or at least the Black Country that lay to its south and east, had an active local aristocracy and a substantial middle class, but the area as a whole was dominated by its large working-class population.[7] Poorly paid, financially insecure and often shoddily housed, they comprised just the sort of market to provide the foundations for a successful career in the drink trade.[8] Some observers drew less charitable conclusions. Across the Black Country, reported the *Edinburgh Review* a year or two before Joseph and Sarah moved to Wolverhampton, 'drunkenness is the direct cause of nine-tenths of all the crimes that are committed'.

Many a man, who in his sober moments is reasonable, industrious, docile, and kind, is changed by drink into something worse than a wild beast; he quarrels with his equals, insults his superiors, and maltreats his family.[9]

These were common enough complaints. But what some saw as evils to be rectified, others, like Joseph, saw as opportunities to be seized, as markets to be satisfied.

Edward's father proved to be a skilled and successful entrepreneur. Although little is known about what he did before he moved to Wolverhampton, it is clear that he embarked upon his career in the West Midlands with few inherited advantages.[10] Very soon after Edward was born in 1867, Joseph was working in the town as a pub tenant.[11] It was a job that involved both hard work and long hours, and even though Sarah and the children lived on the premises, it must have kept Joseph away from them for long periods of time. Whatever the sacrifices he and the family made, they brought their rewards, for within a few years Joseph felt able to describe himself in a local trade directory as 'a wine & spirit merchant, & victualler'.[12]

No doubt, this entry involved more than a touch of hyperbole. But by the time Edward was grown up, such claims were no longer in the least inflated. Despite the onset of more difficult trading conditions,[13] his father prospered, establishing both a wine and spirit business and a chain of licensed premises. He owned four Wolverhampton outlets by 1889–90, seven in 1892, five (including one in Birmingham) in 1894, and seven (all in Wolverhampton) in

1896.[14] Joseph, explained a local newspaper five years later, was 'in a large way of business, and possessed several important establishments in Wolverhampton and elsewhere'.[15]

So it was that when Joseph died in 1901, he left a considerable fortune: an estate valued at over £49,000 – almost £16,000 net.[16] These sums need to be put into perspective. This was at a time when one of Wolverhampton's most senior officials, the town's officer of health, was paid £175 a year,[17] a time when most lawyers and doctors probably earned in the order of £250 a year.[18] This was a time, to put it another way, when it was possible to rent a four-room house for five shillings a week, or to purchase a 'villa' in one of the better suburbs of Wolverhampton for as little as £450.[19]

'Drink, it was in the family' [20]

But economic success did not guarantee social acceptance. Indeed, Joseph and his family's difficulties in this regard draw attention to yet another nineteenth- and early twentieth-century stereotype, that of the self-made businessman struggling to overcome the suspicions of those beyond – and perhaps even within – his immediate economic and social circles. The Lawrence family faced one particular problem in its search for status and respectability: less Joseph's behaviour after the death of his first wife than the way in which he made his money.

Joseph's remarriage within eighteen months of Sarah's death in 1883 was probably not the cause of the gossipy disapproval that it might well be today. Joseph was in his late forties when Sarah died, and as Pat Jalland has pointed out, 'young and middle-aged widowers were strongly encouraged to return to work at an early date, and later to seek solace in a second marriage'.[21]

What was likely to be regarded by many as much more serious was that Joseph and his family were associated so closely with the drink trade. New-won wealth was always suspect, particularly when it was acquired through involvement in the sale of alcohol. Those engaged in the drink trade, especially the more sensitive of them, worried constantly about their respectability. 'To be a "Licensed Victualler" is, as a rule, a guarantee now-a-days of respectability and position', the *Licensed Victuallers' Gazette* reassured its readers in 1880.[22] But there was no denying the *Gazette*'s – and the trade's – anxiety.

> We do not for a moment attempt to argue that every man who keeps
> a public-house is a pattern of all that is good, and that there are
> no flaws to his character; but we do say that, taking the Licensed

Victuallers as a body, they will very favourably compare with any other class of business men in the country.[23]

The Lawrences would never find it easy, then, to shake off the stigma that, in many quarters, attached itself to the way in which they made their money.

The family's first known home in Wolverhampton was the 'Blue Ball', a substantial town-centre pub, well positioned at the corner of two major roads. But it was a pub for all that, and not far from an abattoir.[24] The family continued living in licensed premises until Joseph and Sarah were in their forties, and Edward was in his early teens.[25] When Joseph stood as a Conservative candidate for the town council a few years later, it provided the perfect pretext for the party's opponents to wheel out their anti-drink trade jokes and anecdotes.

> To inform anyone that beer is often adulterated is about equivalent to imparting to them the information that Queen Anne is dead. A short time ago a friend of mine was having a friendly glass with a certain publican who shall be nameless. 'There's something very peculiar and extraordinary about this glass of beer,' said the publican. 'Ah!' remarked my friend, 'perhaps it's a hop.' It took mine host some time to see the joke, and then he didn't appreciate it.[26]

Whatever the trade's reputation for sharp practice, it was as nothing compared to its association with heavy drinking, ill-health and alcoholism. During the early 1880s, for example, male mortality from diseases of the liver stood at 240 per thousand among innkeepers, compared to fewer than 40 per thousand among members of the general population.[27] There were rumours that both Joseph and Sarah had a drink problem. It was common knowledge, apparently, that Edward's younger brother, Robert, drank himself to death when he was just thirty-two years of age.[28] Moreover, it was probably already common knowledge – and certainly would be within a few years – that Edward himself drank heavily, drank publicly and was sometimes seen to be seen 'the worse for drink'.[29] 'Drink,' concluded a police witness at Edward's trial, 'it was in the family.'[30]

'A respectable and respected tradesman'[31]

Despite such barriers to social acceptance, Joseph and his family acquired many of the trappings of middle-class success, status and respectability. As they prospered, they moved, as one might expect, from town-centre public houses to purpose-built homes in Wolverhampton's more desirable suburbs. By the time Edward was in his mid twenties, the family home was a substantial three-storey building almost directly opposite the town's grammar school.[32] Everything about the house spoke to the family's new-found economic success. It was named 'Ashton House', in recognition no doubt of Joseph's Lancashire origins; it was large and imposing, and 'situated in the western suburb of the town, apart from the manufacturing district & in the midst of rural scenery.'[33] Joseph and the family were looked after, in this physical embodiment of their achievements, by three resident servants – an establishment to which relatively few, even middle-class, households were able to aspire.[34]

As he prospered, Joseph became active in the social and political life of the area. The licensed trade had sympathisers as well as opponents, and like many small businessmen, Joseph became a freemason (in nearby West Bromwich).[35] Freemasonry was an organisation which, as Roger Burt explains, enabled men and their families to 'prove their status in the community, mark their progress, and, above all, demonstrate their respectability'.[36] Like many in the licensed trade, Joseph was 'strongly Conservative' in his views.[37] Indeed, with temperance the most important issue in the town's municipal politics,[38] he stood for the council in 1891, his opponents claimed, precisely 'because he was a publican'.[39]

Joseph and a fellow publican John Griffiths took on two sitting Radical-Liberal councillors, G.R. Thorne and S. Larkinson, in the poor 'east end' of the town. Presenting their opponents as temperance supporters, they described themselves as working men's candidates, their popular Toryism drawing upon the pleasures – often far from respectable – of male working-class life. Joseph's election song underlined his, and his party's, identification with both working-class betting and working-class drinking.

> Now if Lawrence and Thorne have a proper fair race
> I will take even money Joe gets the first place.
> When I drink that cold water I get creepy an' pale
> So I'll vote for Joe Lawrence and sparkling warm ale.[40]

The strategy worked. The two Tory publicans were returned, Joseph serving as a town councillor until 1897, and proving, the Liberal *Midland Counties Express* remarked with a distinct lack of enthusiasm, 'a useful member of several important committees'.[41] But it was not a strategy that would work for much longer. Between 1880 and 1914, points out the political historian Jon

Lawrence, 'The typical "Tory working man" of Conservative discourse was transformed from the honest labourer who had earned his right to a quiet pint, to the honest family man who had earned the right to a quiet home life.'[42] This shift in Conservative party rhetoric was a reaction in large part, of course, to the broader changes in gender, class and other relationships that were discussed in the opening chapter of the book. They were changes with which Joseph never needed – and with which Edward never managed – to come to terms.

Like many in the licensed trade, Joseph also took an interest in the local sporting scene. He became a director of Wolverhampton Wanderers, a club that depended heavily, both on and off the pitch, upon local ties and local loyalties. In fact, according to the club's quasi-official historian, 'there was a kind of matiness' in the way that the club was administered.[43] It was a matiness that extended far beyond the pitch. In fact, the relationship between the club and the Conservative party was so close that during the 1892 general election, several Wolves players accompanied Tory politicians on visits to working-class areas of the town, and three years later the entire Wolverhampton Wanderers team attended a local Primrose League demonstration.[44] Joseph's directorship, like his political activity, reflected – and no doubt reinforced – the position that he had attained in Wolverhampton society. For as the president of the Football League explained a few years later, 'In most towns it is considered a distinct privilege to be on the board of the local club directorate, and the position is as eagerly sought after as a seat in the council chamber.'[45]

Joseph's final days attested still more eloquently to his wealth and influence. Seriously ill with dropsy, he was attended to not just by his family doctor, but also by Sir James Sawyer who during the course of a distinguished career held chairs in both medicine and pathology at the University of Birmingham medical school.[46] Joseph's funeral in 1901 provided a fitting tribute to a prominent local worthy. His tombstone was suitably impressive; the 'large attendance of relatives and friends' included two aldermen, three councillors, a representative from Wolverhampton Wanderers, and 'a number of old servants'.[47] Even the politically unsympathetic *Midland Counties Express* was moved to comment both on Joseph's business success and on his good works. 'The deceased gentleman was well known, and was of a generous disposition. He unostentatiously did many kindly and charitable acts in the east-end of the city.'[48] A few years later, in the aftermath of his son Edward's arrest for murder, the town's chief constable remarked pointedly that Joseph had been 'a respectable and respected tradesman.'[49]

3

'A sound English education'[1]

THE LAWRENCES knew the importance of respectability as well as the chief constable – and as well probably as most other people in Wolverhampton. Indeed, the ways in which they brought up their children seem to confirm much of what the existing historiography tells us about the centrality-cum-fragility of Victorian and Edwardian respectability. We have seen that as Joseph became successful, he and his family lived more and more comfortably, acquiring many of the trappings of middle-class prosperity and social standing. But it was a respectability, we have seen too, that was under constant threat, undermined as it was by the family's close association with the drink trade.

The 'Blue Ball'

Joseph and Sarah brought up their children as respectably as they could. Yet, however much they tried to insulate them from the way they made their money, it was an impossible task. Children brought up in public houses such as the 'Blue Ball' were shaped, often profoundly, by the demands of the family business. Edward's father, like publicans everywhere, had to work long hours, liaising with suppliers, deciding whether to employ staff, managing those he did employ, balancing the books, being pleasant with customers and, no doubt, joining them for a drink or two.[2] Edward, like publicans' children everywhere, could not help but see, smell, hear – and hear about – what was going on downstairs or just the other side of the living room wall. Edward, like many publicans' children, grew up knowing that his parents liked a drink – and learning when he was older that his younger brother Robert had developed more than a social liking for alcohol.[3]

Edward's parents, it seems certain, made little effort to challenge prevailing, middle-class attitudes about the separation of the sexes, the inferiority of the working class and the importance of keeping up appearances.[4] The way in which Edward was brought up almost certainly helped to shape his future character and behaviour, and in particular the sorts of relationships that he was inclined to form with the women in his life.

Edward was the eldest surviving son at a time when such things mattered. He had two elder sisters, an elder brother who died when he was three years old, a younger brother and two younger sisters. It seems likely therefore that his parents and siblings (not to mention the octogenarian, paternal grandmother who lived with them while he was little) regarded him – and that he regarded himself – as occupying a special, highly valued place within the family.[5] Edward it was who would be expected, in due course, to take over the running of the family business, to look after his parents and to look out for the interests of his brother and sisters.

The Lawrences, like virtually all middle-class families, organised themselves along conventional gender lines. Edward's father worked, his mother (at least according to the census) did not.[6] It was not just that there were great pressures upon middle-class – and respectable working-class – women not to undertake paid employment.[7] It was also that by the time Edward was four years old, his mother had four children under the age of seven to look after.

Moreover, the Lawrences, like virtually all middle-class – and even some working-class – families, relied upon working-class women for the smooth running of their households. Residential domestic service, it is easy to forget, remained the largest single employer of female labour until well into the twentieth century. In 1871, when Edward was three or four years old, more than 1.5 million women and girls – almost 13 per cent of the female population – were employed in some form of service.[8] Nineteen-year-old Elizabeth Heath was one of this hidden army. She lived with the Lawrences, helping Sarah with the running of the house and the care of the children.[9] It meant that Edward, together with his brother and sisters, grew up living with, and being looked after by, a young woman from a different, and obviously less privileged social and economic background. It meant that the Lawrence children were introduced from the earliest possible age to the basic tenets of contemporary gender and class hierarchies.[10]

These lessons in mid-Victorian power relationships were reinforced by the way in which Edward and his siblings were educated. Joseph and Sarah took care to provide their children with the sorts of schooling that reflected the family's social and economic achievements – and of course its social and economic aspirations. They were careful, for instance, to educate their sons and daughters separately, in segregated, single-sex surroundings.

Joseph and Sarah sent two of their two daughters, Sarah and Jane, to live in Warwick, 'a large and populous town which, from the width of its streets, intersecting each other at right angles, the elegance of its squares, crescents, terraces, parades, and detached villa residences, may vie with any watering-place in the kindom.'[11] They boarded there with a sexagenarian lay assistant missionary from the Pastoral Aid Society,[12] an organisation which had been established during the 1830s to promote 'the maintenance of Curates and Lay-Agents in populous districts'. However, according to K.S. Inglis, 'its unspoken aim was to reproduce in an urban environment the relationship between church and society which its members believed to have been characteristic of an earlier and happier England.'[13] It seems unlikely therefore that the society, or an Irish lay missionary in his late sixties, would do a great deal to encourage Sarah and Jane to challenge conventional, middle-class notions of what was proper and what was acceptable.

Weston School

Joseph and Sarah sent their two surviving sons, Edward and Robert, to board at a private school in Weston on the outskirts of Bath. Weston was one of the town's most desirable residential suburbs, and home to a number of middle-class boarding schools, by reason, it was said, of its healthy situation.[14] Founded like many schools of its type during the 1820s and 1830s,[15] Weston School expanded so that by the time Edward and Robert were pupils during the early 1880s, it had a teaching staff of six schoolmasters, a domestic staff of nine, and approximately 130 pupils. This was a larger and more cosmopolitan group than Edward was used to: the boys, who ranged in age from eight to fifteen, were drawn from all over England, Wales and Scotland – as well as some who lived in countries such as Ireland and India.[16]

There were a number of schools in Bath that restricted their admissions, either explicitly or implicitly, to the sons of 'gentlemen',[17] but Weston did its best to appeal to aspiring middle-class families like the Lawrences. It promised to provide the boys who attended with an education that was at once economical, practical and effective. Its fees, the school's advertising claimed, were 'very moderate'. Its curriculum, it made clear, was geared towards preparing its pupils for modest, but respectable professional and quasi-professional occupations.

The course of instruction is particularly suited to the requirements of Pupils intended to engage in Commercial, Agricultural and manufacturing pursuits. It comprises every branch of a sound English education, including – Book-keeping, Land Surveying, Mathematics, Drilling, Swimming, Shorthand, French, Drawing, Latin, &c.[18]

There was every hope, the school insisted, that in due course the boys who enrolled would be in a position to obtain entry into the sorts of jobs that their parents had in mind for them. Weston School's results, it continued, were highly impressive.

Pupils at this School have been successful at the Following Examinations:- Civil Service, Preliminary of the College of Surgeons, of the Pharmaceutical Society, of the Incorporated Law Society, University Local, College of Preceptors, Science and Art Department.'[19]

The school, like so many catering for the middle-class sector of the market, placed considerable emphasis upon the benefits of sporting activity.[20] For as more than one historian of sport has pointed out, 'Even where extensive playing-fields could not be purchased, the panoply of houses, teams, school colours, songs that surrounded the culture of athleticism were carefully reproduced and proved remarkably successful in attracting the fees of socially ambitious parents of modest means.'[21]

Weston was one of the schools that did have its own grounds, and it organised rugby and cricket matches against local teams.[22] It also set great store by its annual swimming galas and sports days, occasions that afforded obvious opportunities for the school to present itself to the wider world. It did so in more imaginative ways than one might imagine. The 'Aquatic Sports' held in July 1881 included events such as swimming in clothes, diving for twenty eggs, and 'walking the greasy bowsprit'.[23] The sports day held a few weeks earlier included hurdle races, a tug of war, a jockey race, a three-legged race, a 'consolation race (in sacks)' and an obstacle race, which involved climbing up poles, crawling under them, jumping over hurdles and creeping through casks.[24] A band played throughout the afternoon, and the boys were organised in ways that reflected very carefully their standing within the school's various hierarchies. They were grouped not just by age (under nine years old, nine to twelve years old, and twelve to fifteen years old) but by academic aspiration ('Candidates at Oxford Local Examination') and by the position that they held within the school ('Prefects and Monitors').[25]

It is clear then that the education which Edward and his brother received at Weston School reflected, and was designed to reinforce, the conventional, respectable attitudes of middle-class, mid to late Victorian Britain. The intention behind the Victorian cult of athleticism embraced by this and similar schools was to develop in middle-class boys such as Edward and Robert the 'proper manliness' which both parents and teachers felt to be so desirable.

> [T]his redefinition of gender comprised both sexes, establishing new standards of psychological and social normality based on the nuclear family and a firm division of roles between man the master and provider and woman as a kind of exclusively domestic creature whose life was regulated by her reproductive role and the caring duties it entailed.[26]

Whether Edward and his brother conformed or rebelled, whether they accepted or rejected what they were taught, they must have been touched by their time at Weston. The way the school was marketed, the curriculum it offered, the way it was organised, the public face it presented, the boys with whom Edward and his brother lived all tended to buttress the assumptions about gender, class and respectability which were embedded so deeply in the family home back in Wolverhampton.

4

Member of the Royal College of Veterinary Surgeons[1]

WHEN EDWARD LEFT SCHOOL, he trained as a vet, set up in practice, worked abroad and then, while still in his early twenties, moved back to join the family drink business in Wolverhampton. The veterinary profession might seem an unlikely career choice for the son of a publican/wine merchant who was brought up in a midlands industrial town. However, it seems much less strange when one takes into account Edward's parents' aspirations for their sons, the sort of school they sent them to and, not least, the uncertain standing of the veterinary 'profession' towards the end of the nineteenth century.

Veterinary surgery was no job for a gentleman, but it was just the sort of job for a lower middle-class boy looking to make his way in the world. Mid-nineteenth-century veterinary practice, it has been pointed out, was 'not quite a profession'.[2] Despite several attempts to control entry and improve training, veterinary students were not expected to be as highly educated as those training to be doctors.[3] Moreover, most veterinary surgeons continued to face competition from unqualified practitioners, and so found it difficult to earn what they, or most other people, regarded as a comfortable middle-class living. Indeed, according to William Farr's mid-century system of social classification, medical practitioners (including such unlikely figures as corn-cutters and professors of hydropathy) appeared in his Class I, whereas veterinary surgeons (even when they were qualified), were placed in Class IV, alongside those earning their living, far from respectably, as jockeys, farriers, cattle doctors, horse dealers and horse-breakers.[4]

Nevertheless, qualifying as a vet was an expensive business. And although the *Veterinary Record* can scarcely be regarded as a disinterested witness, its calculations provide a useful indication of the sort of investment that the families of those entering the 'profession' were likely to have to make. The journal claimed in the late 1880s, for instance, that trainees needed £500 or so to meet the costs of qualifying and looking for a practice.[5] So it was that despite the gap between aspiration and achievement in so far as their social and economic standing was concerned, veterinary surgeons recognised that it was 'the middle classes, from whence we draw the most of our recruits'.[6]

Edinburgh

Those hoping to qualify as veterinary surgeons could undertake their training in London, Glasgow or Edinburgh,[7] and Edward went to the Scottish capital.[8] Despite its reputation for Presbyterian dullness and dourness, Edinburgh must have struck him as a stylish and sophisticated city.[9] When Edward was a student there during the mid-1880s, it was home to a quarter of a million people, including a university population of well over 3,000. Edinburgh University attracted young men from all over the world: by the time Edward finished his training in 1887, 14 per cent of the faculty of medicine's nearly 2,000 students came from the colonies, with a further 4 per cent from India and 3 per cent from 'overseas'.[10]

Edinburgh's two veterinary colleges, the Royal (Dick) Veterinary College and the New Edinburgh Veterinary College, were small, all-male institutions, and were separate from the university.[11] Nonetheless, the colleges' students shared the undergraduates' reputation for rowdiness and high spirits.[12] Edinburgh's veterinary students, explained the city's *Scottish Leader*, 'were not remarkable for sobriety of demeanour'.[13] Others agreed. 'Student pranks are tolerated to a very trying extent,' concluded a London official of the Royal College of Veterinary Surgeons, 'by reason that they seem to be inevitable.'[14]

Matters came to a head in January 1887, when students from the city's two veterinary colleges jeered and jostled the examiners who had failed a number of candidates during their final-year examinations.[15] The incident escalated, the police became involved, and the press had its say, the ensuing debate ranging wider and wider, from the colleges' recruitment policies to standards of teaching, standards of examining, the state of Anglo-Scottish relations and, not unnaturally, standards of student behaviour.[16]

The controversy revealed, *inter alia*, veterinary students' resentment that they did not necessarily share the gentlemanly status that was routinely ascribed to the city's undergraduates.[17] One Royal Dick student claimed, for example, that he and his colleagues were 'merely a body of young professional gentlemen';[18] a former student, describing himself as 'M.R.C.V.S.', insisted that, 'the student of today … is far more respectable in dress, appearance, and manners than those of twenty-five years ago'.[19] And when the principal of Edward's (New Veterinary) College looked to the future in the wake of the furore, he 'trusted that in the examination before them, no matter what the result, the students would behave, as in the past, like gentlemen'.[20] For as he explained a short while later, the personal and the professional, the manly and the respectable were all intimately entwined.

> I do not think that anyone who does not possess the feelings of a gentleman can appreciate what professional etiquette is, and if I were asked to say what it is, I should say, 'Do unto others as you would others should do unto you.[21]

Whatever the merits and demerits of the detailed arguments that swirled around veterinary training during Edward's time as a student, something was seriously amiss in the way that the system operated. Despite both Edinburgh colleges moving into new, purpose-built premises with lecture rooms, reading rooms, horse boxes and dog kennels, fewer than 15 per cent of their students managed to complete the curriculum within the specified period of three years.[22] In fact, it was revealed during the course of the controversy that between the summer of 1883 and the beginning of 1885, only 30 per cent – 26 out of 86 – of the New Veterinary College's candidates were successful in passing what was known as the 'final board'.[23]

Edward was among the college's more successful students. He passed the examinations set by the Royal College of Veterinary Surgeons in subjects such as science, physiology, histology, and the anatomy of horses and domesticated animals.[24] When he graduated with his diploma, he was entitled – on payment of the appropriate fee – to become a member of the Royal College of Veterinary Surgeons, and to describe himself officially as a 'veterinary surgeon'.[25] In fact, at the annual distribution of prizes and medals held at New Veterinary College in April 1887 Edward was one of twenty students awarded a 'Certificate of Merit for Dressing, Dispensing, and Visiting'.[26]

Shifnal

When they graduated, most newly qualified veterinary surgeons worked for two to three years as an assistant in an established practice before joining a partnership or setting up independently.[27] Edward was one of the minority who was able to open his own practice straight away. He must have had help

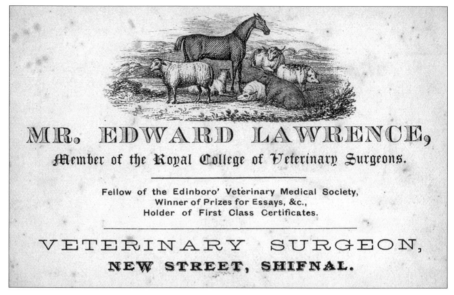

MR. EDWARD LAWRENCE,

Member of the Royal College of Veterinary Surgeons.

Fellow of the Edinboro' Veterinary Medical Society,
Winner of Prizes for Essays, &c.,
Holder of First Class Certificates.

VETERINARY SURGEON,

NEW STREET, SHIFNAL.

Edward Lawrence trained as a veterinary surgeon in Edinburgh, and practised
briefly in Shifnal and Argentina before returning to Wolverhampton in the
early 1890s to work with his father and brother in the family drinks business.
BY COURTESY OF WILLIAM PIGGINS

(presumably from his father). According to advertisements in the veterinary
press at the time he was qualifying in the mid to late 1880s, it cost between
£100 and £200 to purchase a country practice. This was a substantial
investment even when it included, as it often did, a 'horse, trap, drugs and
other professional requisites'.[28]

Whatever backing Edward received, it enabled him to take over an
established practice in Shifnal, a small Shropshire town eight or nine miles
from the family home in Wolverhampton.[29] Once there, he did his best to
behave in ways befitting an aspiring young professional. He practised in one
of the better areas of the town.[30] On his business card he drew attention to
all the educational and professional achievements he could manage to muster.
The town's new vet, he informed potential clients, was not only a 'Member of
the Royal College of Veterinary Surgeons', but also a 'Fellow of the Edinboro'
Veterinary Medical Society, 'Winner of Prizes for Essays, &c., Holder of
First Class Certificates'.[31]

Edward involved himself in the political and social life of the town. He was
one of the small group of Shifnal ratepayers who met in the spring of 1888 to
draw up for the mayor a list of those considered qualified and liable to serve

as constables during the following twelve months.[32] Later in the year, he was a member of the 'well-selected committee' of twelve gentlemen organising the Shifnal Cricket and Tennis Club's invitation dance at the town hall. It was a major event in the town's social calendar. The decorations, for instance, were carefully chosen: 'The orchestra was screened by a tennis net, and the pictures on the walls were relieved with racquet bats, wickets, and cricket balls, the whole presenting a most pleasing effect.' The attendance was respectable and seemingly enthusiastic: 'The ball was patronised by the leading gentry of the neighbourhood, and dancing was kept up until early morn.'[33]

But even taking over an established practice and throwing oneself into local activities were no guarantee of economic and social success. It took time to gain the experience, develop the contacts and secure the reputation upon which the success of a practice depended. 'The best clients are the most difficult to get,' cautioned the *Veterinary Record*: 'consequently a beginner has to put up with those he can find.'[34] Edward, like other formally trained vets, probably faced competition from unqualified practitioners who, despite the Veterinary Surgeons Act of 1881, continued to make use of the term 'veterinary' in their marketing.[35] He certainly faced qualified competition in the form of Lawrence Copeland, who had been practising in Shifnal for at least twenty years.[36] Copeland and his family were deeply embedded in the economic and social life of the town, an involvement that reflected, and no doubt reinforced, Copeland's ability to sustain a substantial, and very possibly loyal, client base.[37]

Even without such direct competition, the economic and social rewards of veterinary practice often proved disappointing. Once established, it is true, qualified veterinary surgeons were able to earn in the order of £150 to £200 a year (about the same, it will be recalled, as Wolverhampton's officer of health).[38] But Edward only stayed in Shinal for two years, and even if his practice proved more successful – more quickly – than most, it was unlikely to bring him the economic and social rewards that he and his family were seeking. Like his rival Lawrence Copeland, Edward was listed in the 'classified trades' section of the county directory, where he found himself competing for attention not just with accountants and solicitors but with an air ball maker, a bill poster, a fishmonger, two milliners, four painters, five tailors and others of similar standing.[39] Edward probably felt a good deal of sympathy with the complaint, which was still being made twenty years later, about the public's widespread failure to recognise that those who had undergone formal training in a veterinary college should be 'entitled to be ranked as a member of an educated profession'.[40]

'Sailing for South America'[41]

Perhaps, too, Edward found Shifnal small and confining. Its main claim to fame, according to the directory in which he and Copeland were listed, lay in the fact that there had been a serious fire there in 1591, 'previous to which the town was of considerable importance'. The directory went on, rather desperately, to elaborate the point. 'A brief was afterwards granted by Queen Elizabeth authorising collections to be made in Salop and adjoining counties to relieve the inhabitants from the deprivations consequent on the conflagration.'[42] Four hundred years later, when Edward opened his practice, the local press routinely referred to Shifnal as 'this quiet little town',[43] reacting with some surprise when 'its normal quietude' was broken by events such as the annual 'Dove club' anniversary or the unexpected arrival of 'excursionists from the black country'.[44]

It is possible, of course, that Edward had other reasons for leaving. Perhaps he had developed a taste for adventure; perhaps he hoped to make his fortune; perhaps he needed to put Shifnal and/or Wolverhampton behind him; or perhaps his parents had some reason for wanting him out of the way. Perhaps, too, his decision to move abroad had its roots in what John Tosh has described as a 'flight from domesticity'. According to this view of events, the empire (informal presumably as well as formal) 'stood for old values and redundant lifestyles'. Such atavism, it is said, could prove enormously attractive. 'The appeal of empire to men might be summed up by saying that it represented an unequivocal assertion of masculinity, a place where autonomy could be achieved without constant negotiation with the opposite sex.'[45]

It was certainly the case that many in Victorian and Edwardian England thought it a good idea for young, middle-class men to spend a period of time abroad. 'It is now regarded as part of the education of a successful commercial man,' remarked the *Licensed Victuallers' Gazette* in 1902, 'that he should travel round the world, or, at any rate, make himself acquainted with the resources, capabilities, and requirements of the British Empire.'[46] Even during the short time that Edward was practising in Shinfal, both the Shropshire press and the veterinary press carried reports extolling the benefits of overseas travel. The *Wellington Standard* printed a letter from a correspondent in Buenos Aires explaining that it was possible for emigrants to do well in Argentina if, like Edward, they were 'young, unmarried men determined to push on, and with the ability to learn the language'.[47]

The *Veterinary Record* also printed editorials extolling foreign travel as the thing 'most likely to widen a man's mind',[48] and promoting the attractions of the Americas, both North and South. There were only two veterinary surgeons in the whole of Brazil, it claimed, so that opportunities there were bound to increase.[49] It couched the attractions of working overseas in what it saw as a telling combination of imperialist destiny and entrepreneurial opportunity.

> Wherever the English-speaking race is to be found there are horses and stock, and there is room for the holder of an English veterinary diploma. In Canada, The United States, The Argentine Republic ... the supply of veterenarians has not yet exceeded the demand.[50]

Whether or not Edward was swayed by such arguments, he left England for Latin America in 1889.[51] It was an opportune time to go, just at the beginning of what was to become known as Argentina's 'golden age'. There were jobs available in stock raising, horse breeding and horse racing,[52] and Edward, it seems, took up a position as a veterinary surgeon, working in what he described later as 'a horse-breeding country'.[53] He was not quite the pioneer he might have imagined. Argentina already had a small British community: the 1895 census recorded 21,000 foreign-born Britons, of whom 6,700 lived in the city of Buenos Aires, and a further 8,700 in the province of the same name.[54]

The British community in Argentina, unlike the Italian, Portuguese or Spanish, was predominantly middle-class, 'with the lead taken by merchants, landowners, engineers and businessmen'.[55] Despite the country's climate, it was possible for those living in this part of South America to enjoy some of the trappings of an English, middle-class way of life. Montevideo, for instance, had its own English club. Buenos Aires had an English-language press (replete with advertisements for Lea & Perrins' Worcestershire Sauce and other British products), and a cricket club (which also held handicap tennis tournaments open to members of its sister clubs in Rosario and Montevideo).[56]

Such faux-Englishness was not enough to keep Edward, who returned to Britain in 1891. It might be more than a coincidence that his homecoming coincided with the economic difficulties precipitated by the Baring Crisis of 1890–91, when the national and provincial authorities in Argentina defaulted on loan repayments to the badly exposed British merchant bank that gave the crisis its name.[57] Although the resulting recession was not severe enough to reverse Argentina's long-term economic expansion, it might well have been sufficient to encourage a bored or dispirited young man to pack up and return to the family home.[58]

Edward never practised again. Nonetheless, he appeared to set some store by his 'professional' training and by his membership of the Royal College of Veterinary Surgeons. He included his veterinary qualifications in his entry in the 1902 edition of the *Court Guide and County Blue Book of Warwickshire, Worcestershire and Staffordshire*,[59] and he never took the trouble to remove his name from the register of the Royal College of Veterinary Surgeons that was published every year.[60] It is possible, of course, that the latter at least was nothing more than an oversight. It seems more likely, however, that the inclusion of the letters 'M.R.C.V.S.' after his name, a decade and more after he last practised, reflected the view that Edward, and probably his family, took with regard to the standing that he had attained, and hoped to continue to enjoy back in Wolverhampton.

5

'Married a respectable person' [1]

WHEN EDWARD RETURNED to Wolverhampton in 1891, his life continued the trajectory typical, it seemed, of an upwardly mobile, respectable young pillar of the community. He began to work with his father in the family business, married a young Black Country woman, set up home and raised a family of four sons and three daughters. However, by the turn of the century or soon afterwards, his life began to assume an altogether different path, albeit one conforming to another well-known stereotype of the times: that of the self-indulgent, uncaring, married philanderer.

'Married life was a happy one' [2]

Whatever the circumstances in which Edward left Argentina, all seemed set fair on his return to Wolverhampton. Young, privately educated, well off and now well travelled, he had everything, one would think, to establish himself successfully in the commercial and social life of the town. He seems to have inherited from his father an aptitude for business that was to stand him in good stead in the years to come. But he also seems to have inherited from Joseph attitudes and interests that were to do him few, if any favours: a conventional, early to mid-Victorian view of marriage; a liking for sport; and an even keener liking for hard drinking.[3] Generous and gregarious when sober, he became, at least towards the end of his life, a very different person 'when in drink, violent and impossible to deal with'.[4]

On his return to Wolverhampton, Edward moved back into the parental home, and joined his younger brother Robert in the family wine, spirit and public house business. Their father set about giving his sons the experience and responsibility they would need in order to be able to take over from him when the time came, making each of them responsible for one of the seven public houses he owned in Wolverhampton.[5] The Lawrence brothers seemed lucky indeed to be associated with such an established, expanding and apparently well-regarded local undertaking.

In fact, by the time Edward returned to Wolverhampton, Joseph, who was now in his mid fifties, had begun thinking seriously about the future of the business. When he made his will in November 1894, he stipulated carefully what he wanted to happen following his death. He appointed two independent trustees, who were to allow Edward and Robert 'to have the general and joint management' of the business. His sons were to continue in charge, 'so long as they manage the said business properly and to the satisfaction of the Trustees and keep proper books of account and submit the same whenever required to the inspection of my Trustees'.

In return, Edward and his brother were each to be paid the sum of £250 a year (and be given first refusal upon any subsequent sale of the business).[6] This was the sort of salary, we saw earlier, that professional men such as lawyers and doctors – and sometimes veterinary surgeons – could expect to earn only once they were well established. So by the mid-1890s, the Lawrence brothers were in a position to plan reasonably confidently for the future. Not only were they working for their father in a successful local business, but they were presumably aware, in broad terms at least, of the plans he had made for it – and for them – in the event of his death.

There were also significant developments in Edward's personal life. Within two years of returning to Wolverhampton, he had married a young West Bromwich woman, Margaret Marion Groom. Slim and attractive, Margaret was regarded apparently as coming from a 'respectable' background.[7] At the time of their marriage, Edward was twenty-six years old and Margaret was nineteen, a reflection perhaps of Victorian men's supposed preference for 'weak, younger women'.[8] In other respects, it must be said, the omens for Edward's and Margaret's life together – and for their future respectability – did not seem terribly auspicious. They were from very different backgrounds: her father was a tailor,[9] and she had worked (despite her apparent respectability) as a barmaid.[10] When they married, in February 1893, it was in a register office, rather than in a church.[11]

> With church marriage reasserting itself in so many places, the civil wedding began to function like the early modern clandestine marriage, providing an alternative for those who wanted a bit of privacy or who could not meet the standards of masculine self-sufficiency and feminine innocence demanded by contemporary standards.[12]

Back in Wolverhampton, Edward Lawrence married Margaret Groom (1874–1955). Edward and Margaret had a large family, but Edward got into 'bad ways', drinking heavily and taking a number of mistresses (including Ruth Hadley). Eventually in 1905, Margaret took the bold and highly unusual step of instigating divorce proceedings against her errant husband.

BY COURTESY OF WILLIAM PIGGINS

However loosely late-Victorian standards of feminine innocence were applied,
Margaret would struggle to meet them. Those who took the trouble to work
it out would conclude that she was almost certainly pregnant when she and
Edward married: their first child, Jeffrey, was born early in October 1893, a
little under eight months after their wedding.[13]

Nevertheless, according to Edward, their early life together was happy.[14]
The newly married couple moved into a substantial family house, close both to
Wolverhampton town centre and to Edward's parents' home.[15] Their marriage,
like his parents', was organised upon conventional gender and class lines, with
Edward the breadwinner and Margaret the homemaker.[16] Indeed, they went
on to have the sort of large, stereotypically 'Victorian' family that by the end
of the century was becoming less and less common in middle-class circles.
Margaret gave birth to five children in eight years: Jeffrey (1893), Harold (1895),
John (1897), Marjorie (1898) and Clement (1900) – and then after a break of
four years, two further daughters, Barbara (1904) and Margaret (1905).[17]

Edward was able to maintain his growing family in comfortable
circumstances. Margaret did not work; and by the end of the century (and

An early twentieth-century view of Wolverhampton, showing Waterloo Road,
the street where Edward Lawrence and his wife Margaret lived for most of
their married life together.

probably before), the family employed two resident staff: eighteen-year-old Winifred Smith who worked as a mother's help/domestic, and sixteen-year-old Ethel Lathe who was employed as a general servant/domestic.[18] They were both young, and like young servants everywhere they could be vulnerable to abuse, violence and sexual exploitation.[19] We do not know whether Edward played any part in hiring Winifred and Ethel, let alone whether he attempted to choose them on the basis of their age, their domestic skills or their sexual attractiveness.[20] During these early years of Edward and Margaret's marriage, there were few signs – perhaps one should say few signs the historian can detect – of the difficulties that lay ahead.

'Came into considerable means'[21]

However, as Edward was to admit later with some understatement, he 'got into bad ways'.[22] The catalyst was almost certainly the death of his father at the end of 1901. When Joseph died, Edward not only lost his father – and his father's possibly restraining influence. He also 'came into considerable means'.[23] According to the terms of Joseph's will, it will be recalled, Edward and his brother assumed joint management of the family business, received salaries of £250 each, and shared equally in the profits from the trust's chain of pubs. It was an inheritance that, in the short term at least, boosted the economic power that Edward had at his disposal and thus his ability, if he so wished, to acquire further symbols of middle-class success and respectability.

The death of his brother less than a year later had less clear-cut consequences. The fact that Robert died – and was known to have died – from heavy drinking can scarcely have enhanced Edward's standing in the local community. But his death probably strengthened Edward's position within the family business because it meant, presumably, that he took over some, if not many, of his brother's responsibilities. It meant, more importantly, that Edward was now Joseph and Sarah's only surviving son, with all that this implied for his, and the Lawrence family's long-term financial prospects.

Whatever the emotional costs of two family bereavements within such a short space of time, they did not seem to diminish Edward's appetite for business. In fact, he decided a few years later that it was time to work for himself. Following a dispute with his father's trustees, he resigned from the position he held in the family business at the beginning of 1905.[24] He purchased a property on the eastern edge of Wolverhampton, turned it into a brewery, and began trading as 'E. Lawrence & Co.' and/or as the 'Midland Brewery'. It was a small firm, employing one clerk in 1906 and two in 1907.[25]

The move into self-employment did nothing to undermine – and may well have enhanced – Edward's reputation as a successful man of business. It was a reputation that survived – apparently distinct from – the reputation he was gaining for his drinking, his womanising and his occasional violence. So it was that when prosecuting counsel was describing Edward at his trial for murder in 1909, he conceded that he 'was a well-to-do, prosperous man, who had held for years a good position in Wolverhampton'.[26] And when the chief constable of Wolverhampton reported what he knew about Edward, he was careful to distinguish between his moral failings and his commercial skills. Although the police had heard a great deal about Edward with regard to the conduct of his private life, 'he has always been a shrewd and able man of business and I have never heard anything against him so far as the conduct of his business has been concerned'.[27]

PART II

SCANDAL

6

'Up to his games again' [1]

E DWARD was prepared to put his respectability – and his marriage – at risk by enjoying, to put it euphemistically, the pleasures that Wolverhampton had to offer. For despite the town's reputation for dullness and provincialism, it was not without its cultural and sporting attractions: an art gallery, for instance, and golf, tennis, cricket and cycling clubs. [2] It also had a good deal to tempt a man, like Edward, with money to spend and a taste for the racy and the unconventional. There were any number of pubs, several music halls and a choice of theatres.

The Grand Theatre, for example, opened in 1894, soon after Edward returned to the town from South America. Its first season included runs of *Sinbad the Sailor* and *The Prodigal Daughter*, a new play involving a re-enactment of the Grand National using six live horses, one of which, it was said, was a former winner of the race. [3] The Empire Palace of Varieties opened in 1898, the year that Edward and Margaret's first daughter was born. The *Express and Star* was entranced: 'The principal entrance from Queen-square leads into a spacious hall, the floors of which are laid with Mosaic, whilst the walls are covered with ornamental glazed tiles. From this hall are arranged the stairs to circle and stalls. A handsome wrought-iron and copper hand-rail has been introduced to this staircase with great effect.' [4]

There was also professional football. Wolverhampton Wanderers had been formed during the late 1870s, and ten years later it became one of the twelve founder members of the football league. [5] The local football club and the local Conservatives, it has been seen, were closely associated, with Edward's father both a director of Wolverhampton Wanderers and a local councillor for the Conservatives. It would not be surprising, then, if Edward shared Joseph's – and many of their fellow Wulfrunians' – attachment to their home-town team. (It would not be surprising, either, if Edward, who like his father ran public houses in working-class areas of the town, had access to and enjoyed several of the other 'pleasures of the people'.[6])

Then there was pigeon shooting, rabbit coursing, dog racing and horse racing, all of which had broad appeal.[7] Middle-class gambling has never received the same attention as aristocratic or working-class betting. But middle-class gambling was more common than is generally supposed – and as 'potentially shaming and reputation-ruining'.[8] A good number of middle-class men enjoyed an occasional flutter, and Edward of course had a veterinary interest in animals. The railway companies organised excursion trips to the bigger events, and Edward attended race meetings as far away as Doncaster.[9] He even invested in the industry, buying shares in the Wolverhampton Race Course Ltd,[10] an outlay which although unlikely to generate high returns, secured him free entry to the company's meetings – and presumably reflected his enthusiasm for the sport.[11]

Once at the racecourse, the certainties of conventional respectability sometimes became very blurred. It was at the races, it has been pointed out, that 'risk and the *risqué* coincided'. As Mike Huggins explains, 'the racecourse may be seen as a liminal area where petty crime was tolerated by both ... the racing and the urban authorities, where a range of popular cultural forms were able to shelter and survive. It provided a pretext for social gathering and cross-class mixing which undermined many reformist mores and fed a climate of anti-bourgeois behaviour.'[12]

Risk and the *risqué* certainly coincided at the Wolverhampton races. In 1891, for example, just as Edward was returning home, the *Licensed Victuallers' Gazette* looked forward excitedly to aristocratic participation in the town's first meeting of the year. 'Lord Dudley is going to entertain a large number of friends for the Dunstall Park races this week. Doubtless we shall see him in the saddle.'[13] Two years later, the Dudley Plate at Wolverhampton was won by the actress – and Prince of Wales's mistress – Lillie Langtry riding under the pseudonym of 'Mr Jersey'.[14]

There is no doubt that Edward's tastes veered towards the racy and the unconventional. He had a group of friends who shared his liking for drinking, gambling and possibly visiting prostitutes.[15] Indeed, it was becoming clear that he drank to excess and that, in the words of the chief constable, he 'lived an immoral life' and engaged in 'immoral conduct with other women'.[16] The key probably lay in Edward's business interests. It was his involvement in the licensed trade that afforded him both the means and the opportunity to indulge his inclinations. It not only rewarded him well and gave him easy access to drink, but brought him into contact with a wide cross-section of local society, including barmaids, a group of mainly working-class women who fostered their 'sexualised identity' for commercial purposes.[17] 'Ladies as a rule do not care to be seen entering a public-house,' conceded the *Licensed Victuallers' Gazette* in 1902,[18] and even women working in the industry recognised, so they said, that, 'the average respectable life of a barmaid only lasted three years'.[19]

Edward's involvement in the licensed trade was also likely to bring him into contact with women who traded still more explicitly upon their sexual identity and availability. Like all towns and cities, Wolverhampton had its prostitutes and its brothels.[20] And those working in the drink trade were more likely than most to know what was going on.

Not only did the brewing industry expand throughout the nineteenth century but also mid-century licensing laws enabled publicans to keep their premises open all day if they so wished. This, according to some, increased the susceptibility of men. In addition, many landlords encouraged prostitution – indeed some pubs doubled as brothels – because of the additional custom it would bring.[21]

Ruth Hadley

Edward was not slow to take advantage. He had sex, we shall see, with a number of women. But by far the most intense and most important relationship of his life was with a young woman named Ruth Hadley. It was a relationship that was to shape – and destroy – both their lives. It led, *inter alia*, to the break-up of Edward's marriage, and to Ruth's death in her mid twenties. It resulted in Edward's trial for murder, and brought about his bankruptcy and subsequent descent into a downward spiral that culminated in his own premature death just a few years after Ruth died.

When Edward and Ruth met in May 1904, they came, very obviously, from strikingly different social and economic backgrounds. Edward was in his late thirties, expensively educated, well spoken, a successful local businessman, with an impressive home, a wife and six children, and a great deal to look forward to. He was confident, sexually experienced, a man of the world who possessed the ability, it was said, to turn on the charm whenever he wanted to.[22]

Ruth was much younger and much poorer, and had already violated virtually every tenet of respectability, male or female, middle-class or working-class. She was twenty-one years old, with something of a temper, and was, it transpired, well able to stand up for herself. 'The daughter of a locksmith,[23] and the niece of a publican,'[24] she was described at the time of her death as five feet five inches or five feet six inches tall, as a 'pretty young woman'[25] and even as 'beautiful'.[26] She had been working as a barmaid, and possibly as a prostitute.[27] Indeed, her life may have been at something of a crossroads. According to Edward's defence counsel at his trial for murdering her, when they met, Ruth 'was sleeping on a plank bed in a common lodging house, and was living an immoral life'.[28]

The pair had few compunctions about getting involved with one another. Edward probably saw Ruth as another young, working-class woman ready for seduction. Ruth saw Edward perhaps as a middle-aged 'nob', with more money than sense, who might be persuaded to provide her with some sort of meal ticket.[29] She told him something about herself, and explained, according to Edward's account of events, 'what she was afraid of drifting into'.[30] He denied seducing her,[31] but as soon as they met, he took her to Birmingham, where they spent the night together.[32]

This was more than a one-night stand. Edward, it seems, was smitten. Throwing caution to the winds, he appeared unconcerned about jeopardising his, and his family's, hard-won respectability. Almost immediately, he took rooms for his new mistress, and began providing for her.[33] Indeed, between the summer of 1904 and the end of 1908 their relationship settled into a pattern – if pattern is the word for so chaotic an arrangement – that was characterised by a seemingly endless round of arguments, separations and reconciliations.

Their affair must soon have become common knowledge. Within a few months of their meeting, Edward had installed Ruth in Wolverhampton. He found her accommodation just half a mile or so from the family home which he still shared – at least some of the time – with Margaret and the children. Edward divided his time between his wife and his mistress, managing to get both of them pregnant within just over a month of one another during the course of July and August 1904.[34] Calling herself Mrs Fenn and passing herself off as Lawrence's wife, Ruth lived in her new home until the middle of October 1904.

Edward was becoming more and more reckless. We do not know when he told Margaret – or that she guessed – about his relationship with Ruth. But he never seemed to make much effort to keep the affair a secret. In December 1904, when both his wife and his mistress were four to five months pregnant, he moved Ruth even closer to the family home. She stayed there until the middle of 1905, again masquerading as his wife, but this time choosing – less imaginatively – to call herself Mrs Smith.[35] As if this was not all provocation enough, Edward left his wife and children at home for a fortnight so that he could take his mistress away for a holiday at Borth on the Welsh coast.[36]

The relationship between Margaret and Ruth, like that between Margaret and Edward, is difficult to disentangle. The problem is that Margaret appears, superficially at least, to be something of a cipher. She emerges from many of the sources we have at our disposal as a one-dimensional figure, the sort of person to whom, during much of her marriage, bad things happened. She was betrayed by her husband, treated with contempt by his mistress, left to look after her young family, and no doubt pitied and/or ridiculed by the growing number of people who knew what was going on.

But Edward's and Margaret's relationship was by no means as one-sided as it might seem. Margaret did sometimes take the initiative. On one occasion, for instance, she called on Ruth, and urged her to put an end to the affair. She asked her to give up Edward and lead a better life; Ruth refused, explaining that Edward gave her everything that she wanted.[37] It is hard to see that the confrontation did much to help any of those involved. This *menage à trois*, like so many before and since, had more losers than winners. Margaret was the victim, but possibly found it difficult to avoid blaming herself, at some level, for what was happening to her marriage. Edward had the lover he wanted, but he had to support two households, at the same time as dealing with two pregnant women, the births of two children by two different women, and the interest, presumably highly prurient, of those familiar with the state of his marriage. Ruth too had the lover she wanted, but she must have been perfectly well aware of the moral, economic, social and cultural pressures that were always going to threaten to tear them apart.

The spring of 1905 was particularly difficult. Edward resigned from his position in the Lawrence family firm. Edward and Margaret's daughter, Margaret, was born at the end of March, Edward and Ruth's daughter, Dorothy, at the beginning of May.[38] Edward dealt with the former by leaving the baby with Margaret, and with the latter by sending the baby to live with Ruth's sisters.[39] Edward's pleasure-seeking knew few bounds. Within a month of the birth of his and Ruth's daughter, he almost certainly spent the night at a nearby brothel.[40]

Divorce

Edward's conduct had a devastating impact upon his marriage. But the final straw was probably his violent behaviour. According to Margaret, matters came to a head on Good Friday 1905, less than a month after the birth of their daughter, and just two weeks before the birth of Edward and Ruth's daughter. Margaret's relationship with her husband had deteriorated to such an extent, she claimed, that Edward threatened to kill her, striking her 'a violent blow' on the forehead with a stick.[41]

Then, towards the end of July, he attacked her again. Margaret was in the kitchen shelling peas with a servant and her sister when Edward came in, and hit her on the side of the head. He then followed her outside, hitting her several times more until she sought 'protection at a neighbouring house'. The doctor who examined her later in the afternoon confirmed that she had been struck on the cheek and the jaw, and that her right eye was beginning to become discoloured. Indeed, when Margaret confronted Edward later still in the day, he threatened, it was said, to 'break her * * * jaw'.[42]

It was Edward's second attack on her, and Margaret was no longer prepared to be his supine victim. She not only confronted her husband but, following police intervention, went on to appear at Wolverhampton Police Court six days later. In a hearing that resounded to the sound of gender, religious and class sensitivities being affronted, Edward was charged with assaulting and threatening Margaret. Whatever else respectable, manly, middle-class men got up to, they did not hit their wives, they did not hit them on a Sunday, and they did not hit them in front of the servants or other members of the family.

Although it was said that Margaret was reluctant to press charges, the case came to court, explained prosecuting counsel, because it was of such a serious nature. 'The assault took place on Sunday, and he felt bound to say was not provoked by Mrs Lawrence – on the contrary, it came upon her as a surprise.' Reluctant or not, Margaret proved a demurely eloquent witness. She took the stand, her eye still blackened, to confirm what had happened, adding that she 'had been afraid of the defendant for a long time'. She was able to make it clear, both by her words and by her appearance, that Edward's drinking, promiscuity and violence had violated virtually every tenet of manly, middle-class respectability.[43]

There was not much that Edward's counsel could do. He admitted that his client had attacked Margaret, explained that if Edward 'could undo what he had done he would very gladly do so', and promised that he 'was willing to make a most liberal provision for Mrs Lawrence and the children'. Above all, he did his best to stress the respectability of Edward's background. 'Defendant was a man of good position; he was the son of an old tradesman, and the incident was a matter of very great regret and sorrow to him.'

The stipendiary magistrate was not impressed. He was exercised as much, it seems, by Edward's failure to behave properly in front of his servants and extended family as he was by the violence that he had meted out towards his wife: 'It was a serious, cowardly, and disgraceful assault upon a wife in the presence of two servants and his wife's sister.'[44] He was affronted, too, by the immunity he feared that Edward's financial position would afford him: 'It was no use inflicting a pecuniary penalty, that would be no punishment to a man in his position.' The stipendiary decided therefore to sentence Edward to a month's imprisonment with hard labour (for assaulting Margaret), and to bind him over to keep the peace for six months (for threatening her). He was later persuaded, however, that these punishments were unduly severe. 'He thought that the defendant deserved every day of the sentence that had been passed, but it frequently happened that sending one person to prison inflicted punishment on others, and ... if Lawrence went to prison it would inconvenience others.' He therefore reduced Edward's punishment to a fine of £5 plus costs.[45]

Margaret had challenged Ruth; she had confronted Edward; and she had now given evidence against him in court. What she did next removes any lingering doubts as to her resilience, her determination – and no doubt the family support that she was able to draw upon. Deciding that she had no choice but to leave Edward, she not only took the children with her to stay at her father's house in Birmingham, but she also began, in a bold and highly unusual step, to instigate divorce proceedings against her errant husband. Margaret was one of just 400 or so women a year who filed petitions for divorce during these early years of the twentieth century.[46] It took an exceptional woman to do such a thing: even though the Matrimonial Causes Act had been on the statute book for almost fifty years, ending a marriage by divorce remained expensive, inconvenient and inequitable.[47]

Whether or not Edward had deliberately engineered Margaret's departure, he was quick to take advantage of it. Within two days of Margaret leaving the family home, he moved Ruth in. This was another truly remarkable step. It was one thing to keep a mistress conveniently close to hand; it was another thing altogether to install her in one's own house, for neighbours, friends, acquaintances and passers-by to see. Whether the move was a sign of the couple's growing recklessness, their growing contempt for Margaret and her family, or their growing commitment to one another, it did little to improve the volatility of their relationship.

Edward continued to wield the economic power, Ruth, it seems, the emotional sway. It was Edward, Ruth was never allowed to forget, who paid for the house they were living in. It was Edward who was responsible for paying the bills and employing the staff (including as his caretaker Isabella Pickett, Ruth's neighbour in whose house she had given birth). It was Edward therefore who decided whether, on what terms, and for how long his mistress was allowed to stay with him. But Ruth, as one would expect, found ways of retaliating, persuading Edward to behave, or allow her to behave, as she wanted. She shouted, she swore, she threatened, she was prepared to be violent (and as will be seen below, she found ways of manipulating her relationship with Isabella).[48]

It seems to have been Edward's choice that he and Ruth had separate bedrooms, and slept together only some of the time.[49] It was certainly Edward's choice to get Ruth to leave the house in September 1905, less than two months after he had moved her in. But he was unable to prevent her coming back. While he was out one day, Ruth persuaded Isabella – or persuaded Isabella to tell Edward she believed – that she and Edward had been reconciled, and that Edward had 'ordered' her to return to the house. When Edward came back to find that Ruth had moved back in, he told Isabella in no uncertain terms that she must never again allow Ruth into his home. Meanwhile, Ruth took the opportunity to go upstairs, smashing an ornament in Edward's room and, in a telling gesture, destroying two of Margaret's hats which were in a box in the nursery.[50]

Edward and Ruth patched up their differences, Ruth fetching her things and beginning to sleep at the house on a regular basis. But she and Edward continued to quarrel. On one occasion when Edward was on his way to Doncaster races, he sent a cabman to collect his travelling bag. Ruth refused to let him have it and then, changing her mind, gave it to him, supposedly saying, 'I hope the train will run off the line and smash him.' When Edward returned home the following evening at about a quarter to eleven, he accused Ruth of being drunk and refused to sleep with her. She retaliated by accusing him of going with other women, and then during the night confronting him with the revolver that he kept under his bed. Threatening to blow his 'brains out', she was restrained only by the combined efforts of Edward, who distracted her, and Isabella Pickett who pinned her by the throat and pushed her back onto her bed. Ruth, explained Isabella later with some understatement, 'was a very passionate and violent woman in drink'.[51]

Edward's relationship with Ruth was possibly complicated by his resignation from the family business at the beginning of the year. It must have been complicated still further during the final three months of the year as Margaret's petition for divorce made its expensive – and no doubt embarrassing

– way through the legal system. Finally, on 15 January 1906, he and Margaret appeared at the Royal Courts of Justice in the Strand. Edward did not defend the suit, and Margaret obtained a decree *nisi* against Edward on the grounds of his 'Adultery coupled with cruelty towards the petitioner'.

The decree was never made absolute, so although Edward and Margaret lived apart they remained legally married.[52] Nonetheless, theirs was a *de facto* if not a *de jure* divorce. Margaret was granted custody of the children. Edward agreed to move out of the family home, allowing Margaret and the children to live there. He was also required by the court to meet the costs of the case, and to pay Margaret 'alimony pending suit' of £2 10*s*. 0*d*. per week, together with £20 'in respect of arrears pending enquiry'.[53] His marriage was over and so, one imagines, were any lingering claims he may have had either to conventional respectability or to most forms of middle-class manliness.

7

'Addicted to drink' [1]

S o, by the beginning of 1906, Edward was free: free of Margaret, free of her family, free of the children, and free therefore of the few remaining restraints upon his increasingly volatile and disreputable behaviour. It seems doubtful, though, whether he saw his new-found independence in quite these terms. His marriage had not noticeably reined in his activities, and his 'divorce' seemed to make things more, rather than less, difficult with Ruth. Their relationship continued to be characterised, as it had before the divorce, by spells of domestic harmony punctuated by bitter quarrels and acrimonious separations. The difference now was that the periods of harmony appeared to be getting shorter, the quarrels more unpleasant and the separations more prolonged. The three years between Edward's divorce in January 1906 and Ruth's death in December 1908 saw their lives spiralling, if not out of control, then inevitably, it seems, towards some sort of traumatic denouement.

Edward's resignation from the family firm at the beginning of 1905 ended neither his association with the drink trade nor his opportunities for getting to know the women who worked in it. His new enterprise, known variously as the 'Midland Brewery' and 'E. Lawrence & Co.', was small, and like many small breweries it not only supplied beer but owned, or had interests in, a number of local public houses.[2] Given what we know about Edward, it would not be surprising if he was tempted to take less care in managing the production process than in visiting the outlets with which the firm had connections.[3]

'I'll blow your brains out' [4]

However assiduous Edward was in pursuing his business interests, he was soon spending a good deal of time at the Victoria Hotel in Wolverhampton. The attraction was Lottie Davis, a widow who, it was said, was earning 'a respectable living' as manager of the vaults. Whatever her scruples, she and Edward became lovers, with the result, perhaps inevitably, that she was dismissed from her job. Edward did what he could, finding her lodgings and then making her manageress of one of the public houses he owned, the Perrott Arms Hotel in Oldbury.[5] It was at this same time, Edward explained later, that he and Ruth 'drifted apart'.[6]

But he was clear neither of Ruth nor of Lottie. His relationship with Ruth resumed what was its normal course, except that Margaret and the children were now living in the family home and Edward began leading a peripatetic existence around Wolverhampton's inner suburbs. Ruth came round to one small house he was renting, and – in a fit of drunkenness, claimed Edward – either sold his furniture or gave it away.[7] Edward moved to another house; he and Ruth were reconciled; and she moved back in with their baby Dorothy.

Inevitably, it seems, they quarrelled again. But Ruth's family was never far away. Working-class families tended to live near one another, to see one another and to look out for one another.[8] So whatever Ruth's family felt about her relationship with Edward, they were prepared to provide her with help when she needed it. When Ruth left Edward in November, she took the baby to her cousin Frederick Williams, who was working as a press tool maker. Later the same evening, she and Frederick returned to see Edward, her cousin serving, incongruously, as a nursemaid-cum-bodyguard. When they arrived at Edward's house, Frederick stood at the gate with the baby, while Ruth knocked on the door. Edward answered it, revolver in hand.

'What do you want?' demanded Edward. 'Go back with your bloody bully where you have been.'

'I shan't go; I want to come in.'

'If you are not off, I'll blow your brains out.'

Ruth and her cousin left, but Ruth returned a little later, this time adopting a more maternal – and more effective – tack.

'If you won't have me in,' she pleaded, at least 'give me the baby's food.'

Edward did so, but still would not let her in, and Ruth had no option but to spend the night with Frederick and his wife.[9]

'Brewer and widow'[10]

Edward found it no easier to sever his ties with Lottie. Towards the end of November, she wrote to him telling him that she was pregnant. She pleaded for his support, both emotional and material.

I have learnt to love and your treatment to me has wounded me beyond description. I am dependent upon you since I lost my place. Immorality among manageresses will not be [s]tood by brewery companies, and my own people have all turned from me.[11]

Edward was unmoved, believing – or affecting to believe – that he was not the father of the child. Lottie wrote to him again, complaining that he 'had attached more importance to the words of a discharged servant against her mistress than the woman who had loved him and never deceived him'.[12]

Edward was furious. He went to Lottie's house in West Smethwick and, according to her account of events, 'assaulted her without the slightest provocation'. The following day, he visited her at work, ordered her out of the bar, and demanded that she hand over the keys to the safe. She responded by taking out a summons for assault: he retaliated a few days later by laying a charge of larceny against her.[13] It was the first of many occasions over the next few years that Edward was prepared – it almost appears eager – to pursue his grievances through the courts.

The two cases came to trial early in 1907. The proceedings bordered on the farcical: Lottie withdrew her summons for assault; and Edward's cross-summons charging her with stealing £4 0s. 8d. was adjourned for two weeks. But this was not before the nature of their relationship was laid bare for all to see.[14] When the court reconvened, Edward's counsel admitted immediately that the case should never have been brought. There was no case against Lottie, and he did not propose to offer any evidence against her. Nonetheless, he maintained that he owed it to the bench to explain the circumstances leading to the dispute. The money alleged to have been stolen was 'merely a question of book-keeping'. At worst, Lottie had been guilty of carelessness: 'An examination of the books showed that on some occasions she had debited herself with too much and on other occasions with too little.' Edward and Lottie, counsel concluded, should have settled the matter between them. The magistrates, not surprisingly, dismissed the case against her.[15]

However indifferent Edward was to local opinion, he cannot have enjoyed the publicity surrounding the case. Two of the newspapers published in Wolverhampton, the *Express and Star* and the *Midland Counties Express*, carried virtually identical reports of the hearings. The stance they took can be gauged from the headlines over their stories: 'Brewer and Widow. A Charge that Failed at Oldbury';[16] and 'Brewer and Lady Friend. Remarkable Revelations. A Wolverhampton Defendant.'[17] The innuendo continued:

Attired in a smart brown costume, with a chic picture hat of the same shade, Mrs Lottie Davies appeared at the Oldbury Police Court this [Tuesday] morning charged with having stolen £4 0s. 8d. The defendant is a widow, residing at St Paul's-road, West Smethwick; and until recently she was manageress of the Terrott Arms Hotel, Birmingham-road, Oldbury. She had been placed in that position by Mr Edward Lawrence, a Wolverhampton brewer, who had made the acquaintance of the lady whilst she was a barmaid at the Victoria Hotel, Wolverhampton.[18]

'A long and searching cross-examination'[19]

What Ruth made of all this we do not know. What we do know is that she and Edward got together again some time during the spring and summer of 1907, but that in September he ejected her from the house for what he thought would be the final time. With Ruth out of the way, Edward installed as his 'housekeeper' Emma Stacey, another young woman with whom he had had an affair and fathered a child.[20] Ruth was furious. She attacked Edward and then, in what she obviously regarded as an act of considerable symbolic importance, she 'brought away her photo'. Edward, in turn, responded in a way designed, it seems, to upset her as much as he could: he sent her a letter saying that if she did not return the picture he would take steps to prosecute her.[21]

This was possibly no idle threat. In all events, the publicity that Edward had received in the Lottie Davis case did not deter him from further recourse to the law. This, though, was a very different case. In October 1907, just nine months after his relationship with Lottie had been paraded in open court, he charged one of the clerks working at his brewery with fraud and embezzlement.[22] The sums involved were modest – 8s. 6d., 11s. and £2 5s. 4d. But the consequences for Edward proved, once again, to be profound and humiliating.

He was subjected to what one local paper described, without an iota of exaggeration, as 'a long and searching cross-examination'. The questioning drew upon virtually every aspect of Edward's disintegrating respectability: his commitment to work, his liking for drink, and his treatment of women.

'Were you personally attentive to your business?' demanded counsel for the accused clerk.

'I do not quite understand you,' replied Edward.

'Do you consider yourself a business man?'

'I have that reputation.'

However, he admitted when pressed that he did not always supervise very closely his clerk's handling of the firm's money. But this was nothing compared to what was to follow.

'Are you a sober man?' counsel continued.

Lawrence turned to the recorder: 'I appeal to you, sir; is this a proper question?'

The recorder, 'Yes, perfectly.'

Counsel repeated his question: 'Are you a sober man?'

'A sober as most men go.'

'Are you addicted to drink?'

'As most people, I am not a teetotaller. I think I am being insulted.'

He appealed again to the recorder, but the cross-examination was allowed to continue.

'Are you addicted to drink?' repeated counsel.

'Do you ever get drunk?, added the recorder.

'No, sir. Am I being tried for my morals?'

Edward might have thought that the questioning could not get any more embarrassing. But it did.

'Have you been divorced from your wife?'

'No.'

Counsel changed tack once again, this time producing a press cutting of the proceedings at Oldbury police court, 'in which witness appeared to have taken proceedings against a lady who had been a manageress'.

'I am not responsible for what the press say,' retorted Lawrence.

Counsel persisted: 'Will you say that no summons was taken out against Mrs Davies?'

'As far as I remember, no.'

The recorder: 'Was a summons ever taken out against her?'

'It was in prospect; but as far as I remember, no.'

It was only when counsel began asking Lawrence questions about assaulting his wife that the recorder finally decided to intervene: 'I don't see how the witness's treatment of his wife affects this.'[23]

The damage done to Edward's reputation, one imagines, was both deep-seated and irrevocable. Of course, it is never possible to assess precisely the impact that the reporting of court cases – or of anything else – has upon public opinion. But on this occasion it seems safe to assume that if the trial had any effect, it was to reinforce the impression that Wulfrunians were already gleaning about Edward's character and behaviour. It would be difficult for readers of the *Express and Star*, for example, to miss the headline, 'Alleged Embezzlement: Prosecutor under a Warm Cross-Examination', or to overlook the sub-headings beneath it, 'Are My Morals in Question?' and 'Purgatory on Earth'.[24]

'Quarrels between Lawrence and Hadley'[25]

By this time, too, Edward's and Ruth's behaviour had brought them to the attention of the authorities. There was the occasion, it was said, when Edward bit off a policeman's buttons and pushed him down a manhole.[26] There was the occasion, it was reported, when he was accused of biting a policeman's thumb, but got 'away with a fine and a severe dressing-down by the Bench'.[27] There were other incidents, too: 'the police have been frequently called to quarrels between Lawrence and Hadley and on several occasions both have been the worse for drink.'[28]

Edward and Margaret's divorce must also have been more-or-less common knowledge in the town, and probably a local *cause célèbre*. It is difficult now to appreciate quite how unusual, and quite how shaming, it was for a marriage to end in this fashion. Divorce was expensive, and even women wealthy enough and self-confident enough to consider such a step had to be able to prove not only their husbands' adultery but also that it had been aggravated by cruelty or desertion.[29] The result, we have seen, was that Margaret was one of only 400 or so women throughout the whole of England and Wales who filed petitions for divorce each year at the beginning of the twentieth century.[30] If Edward and Margaret's divorce was not public knowledge before Edward took his clerk to court, it became so as soon as he did.

Between Edward moving Emma Stacey in with him in September 1907 and shooting Ruth Hadley in December 1908, Edward and Ruth's relationship assumed a still more rancorous course. There was the provocation of Edward's relationships with Lottie Davis and Emma Stacey. There was the fact that he continued to be involved with his ex-wife and children. In the spring of 1908 he enrolled all three of his sons, John, Harold and Geoffrey, in Wolverhampton Grammar School, a commitment costing a total of £5 10s. a term (assuming that he took advantage of the 1901 discounts available for second and third brothers).[31] It was Edward, it seems almost certain, who footed the bill: he was in the habit of sending one of his servants round to Margaret's house every Friday afternoon with money for his estranged family.[32] And all three boys were removed from the school just a year after enrolling, and this at the very time that Edward had to meet the costs of defending himself against the charge of murdering his lover.[33]

Although Edward was now living with Emma Stacey, he was unable or unwilling to sever his ties with Ruth; and although Ruth had been displaced by another woman, she was unable or unwilling to abandon her relationship with Edward. Indeed, the former lovers saw one another much more often than one might expect. Edward continued to employ Ruth, from time to time, as a servant – in the very house where Edward and Emma were living together. Ruth continued to confront Edward whenever and wherever she was able to engineer a meeting. It was a combustible combination, laced liberally – and ultimately fatally – with drink, jealousy, desire and resentment.

Thus, by the beginning of 1908 Edward was known, and known widely one imagines, for his drinking, his promiscuity and his disdain for conventional respectability. Ruth's behaviour was probably less well known. The problem is that the evidence we have about Ruth nearly all emanates from Edward's defence team at his trial for murdering her. According to their version of

Another early twentieth-century view, this time of Queen Square in the centre of Wolverhampton. The postcard shows one of Edward Lawrence's public houses, the Board Inn (with the name 'Lawrence' prominently displayed). Edward returned to the Board Inn following his acquittal of murdering Ruth Hadley, and gravitated there time and time again during the time that he lived in the town.

events, she was known, to friends and acquaintances at least, for her drinking, her stormy relationship with Edward and her readiness to resort to violence and the threat of violence.[34] It was said, for example, that she smashed a window at one of Edward's public houses, the Board Inn in the centre of Wolverhampton; and it was alleged that she was sacked from another pub, the Coach and Horses in Selly Oak, for trying to throw a fellow barmaid through a window.[35]

Ruth seems to have turned her aggression on to Edward. She told one acquaintance that she had threatened him with a revolver, and tried to flood his house with beer.[36] She told another that she had cracked his skull with an umbrella, had 'lodged a hole' in his leg with a stair rod, and had hit him in the eye with a bottle, making 'a hospital job of it'. She would not, she was reported as saying, allow him go back to his wife and children. 'I will make him crawl for mercy at my feet … He will either kill me or I shall kill him.'[37]

She started going to the Chequer Ball Inn, the public house whose licence Edward's father had entrusted him with when he returned to Wolverhampton in the early 1890s. Once there, she would wait in the yard for her lover to appear. On one occasion, she apparently boasted to the pub's manager, 'Have you heard about him? I have struck him with a bottle of wine. You should see his face.' When the manager warned her to be careful, she allegedly retorted, 'I don't care. I intend to kill the * * * before long. I don't care what becomes of me.' He did not think to warn Lawrence about Ruth's threats because, he explained, 'This sort of thing was quite common talk.'[38]

Ruth also started going to Edward's new home, which was slightly further from the centre of town than where he had been living previously. However, the distance proved little deterrent. Neighbours saw them quarrelling, saw her brandishing a knife, and saw her kicking at the front door in an effort to get into the house.[39] Then towards the end of October 1908, she called on Edward with her sister, Theresa.[40] Ruth was angry because, she claimed, 'He has been up to his games again.' However, her grievances were financial as well as emotional. When they arrived at the house, Ruth asked Edward for the money he owed her for the work she had done. He replied that he did not have any. She asked him again. The altercation escalated.

'You will get none,' he insisted.

'I should like to hit you.'

'I will leg you.'

When Theresa turned round, she noticed, she claimed, that Edward was holding a revolver in his hand.

'Don't shoot her. Had I known you had been quarrelling I would not have called to see you for the world.'

Walking out of the room, Ruth turned to her sister: 'He has already shot at me twice now.'

'Surely Mr Lawrence, you don't mean to say you would shoot Ruth, do you?' demanded Theresa.

'No, Mrs Harriman, I love your sister.'

'It's fine love when you threaten to shoot her.'

'I am only doing it to frighten her. They are only blank cartridges.'

As Ruth came back into the room dressed in her outdoor clothes, there was a knock at the door. Theresa, who was nearest, opened it: 'Thank God, it's a policeman.'

'What has been the matter here?' asked the constable (whom Edward had almost certainly sent for to get rid of Ruth).

'I want this woman out of this house,' said Lawrence pointing to his lover.

'She is coming, officer, now with me,' intervened Theresa. 'Before I go, you understand, Mr Lawrence, I have witnessed the lot. Show the officer what you have behind you.'

Somebody (Edward presumably) had ordered a cab. When it arrived, the two sisters made for the door, Ruth hitting Edward in the face with her handbag as she left.[41] Theresa was crying and Ruth, according to the cabman, was 'helplessly drunk'. Indeed, when they arrived at Theresa's house, Ruth was in such a state, the cabman claimed, that he had to pull her out of the cab by her legs.[42] But the next day, it seems, she was back living with Edward.[43]

Meanwhile, Edward was getting ready to move yet again, a pattern of behaviour which (as with working-class 'flitting') must have undermined his reputation for reliability and respectability. Towards the end of 1908, he began renting 2 George Street, a building that was to loom large in subsequent events. Part of a Georgian terrace, it was more imposing than his existing house, closer to the town centre and closer as well to several of the public houses that he needed to visit.[44] But it needed redecorating.[45] The painting, plastering and wallpapering were finished by the end of October,[46] and Edward moved in with Emma Stacey during early to mid-November. It was a seemingly respectable household. Edward and Emma, like Edward and Ruth before them, lived together as man and wife, but in this case kept their young child with them.[47] 'Miss Stacey was head of the house', and Edward employed two servants, Ethel Cross and Kate Maddox, who were joined in the middle of December by a third, Elizabeth Wardle.[48]

This was all too much for Ruth. Edward's new domestic arrangements – together perhaps with the onset of Christmas – brought matters to a head. Ruth was spending a good deal of time in the town centre, often, it seems, on the lookout for Edward. A week before Christmas, she found him, accosting him with the words, 'You *** swine, I will swing for you yet.'[49] Asked shortly afterwards how she was 'getting on with Teddy now?' her reply was threatening, but probably more with bravado than with genuine menace: 'There will be no Teddy when I have done with him.'[50]

Meanwhile Edward's domestic arrangements were beginning to unravel. He 'was drinking heavily', and three days before Christmas, the servants heard him threaten Emma Stacey: 'If you don't keep quiet,' he said to her, 'I will quieten you for good.' What happened next provides an illuminating insight into the balance of power that might exist even within the seemingly tightly controlled environment of the middle-class household. 'Employers expected obedience, meekness, deference and competence in those who performed personal services.'[51] But they did not necessarily get what they wanted. Servants, we have seen, 'had their own methods of revenge against unfair treatment, using familiar weapons such as sulking, mis-hearing orders, semi-deliberate spoiling of materials, wasting time, "the sullen dumb insolence and petty irritations" bemoaned by employers.'[52] So although domestic servants are commonly held to be among the most deferential and compliant of all workers, there were some who were prepared to challenge their subordination and react in ways that reflected gender, and possibly class, loyalties.[53]

Edward's servants were certainly not compliant. When he threatened Emma Stacey with quietening her 'for good', the servants sided with their mistress – and all four women left the house. We do not know, of course, how far the servants were motivated by fear of Edward and how far by friendship with Emma. But whatever the personal relationships that had developed within George Street, the servants' decision to walk out meant that they sided with the female, presumably working-class 'head of the house' against the male, middle-class 'master' who employed them and paid their wages. However one interprets their action, it cuts sharply across the stereotype of the isolated, subservient and defenceless servant that is embedded so strongly in our understanding of the Victorian and Edwardian period.

As if to emphasise the servants' independence, Elizabeth Wardle returned to George Street the day after they left, saying that she had forgotten her slippers and pocket handkerchiefs. Edward allowed her go upstairs to look for them in the 'top-room'. But this was almost certainly a pretext to enable her to look for his revolver in order, presumably, to prevent him shooting

Emma Stacey, himself or anybody else. Elizabeth found it, loaded, under a pillow in Edward's bedroom. She took it home with her, and the next day, Christmas Eve, she arranged for somebody to discharge it for her in the garden of her home.

It was also on Christmas Eve that Edward and Ruth met again, while he was in the town centre visiting his pubs to make sure that everything was in order. This meeting was more amicable than usual, Ruth asking him who he had with him in the house, and what he would be having for his Christmas dinner. Edward replied that he was living alone, and that he did not know what he would be eating the next day. Ruth saw her opportunity.

'Can I come and cook your Christmas dinner for you?'

'No; I won't have you in the building.'

According to Edward, she begged to be allowed to stay over the holiday and promised that if she did, she would not have a single drop to drink. 'In a weak moment', he agreed, and gave her one of the two latch keys to the house. He was cautious, though. Knowing Ruth so well, he explained, he looked for his revolver as soon as he got back to George Street, but could not find it. He later discovered that 'the girl Wardle' had taken it with her the previous day. He sent 'someone' to collect it, reloaded it, and put it back under the bed.[54]

At about 4.30 in the afternoon, Ruth called to see her sister, Kate Lewis, and together they made their way back to George Street. Kate's account of what happened on their return presented Ruth and Edward's relationship with one another in a reassuringly positive light.[55] 'I helped her to clean up the house.' 'No other girl was then in the house.' Ruth had not been drinking, claimed Kate, whereas Edward, who came home about 7.30, 'wasn't sober'. In fact, 'he was very drunk'. But there was no arguing or unpleasantness. He 'was talking to my sister in a friendly way and I left them … friendly.' In fact, it seems that by the time Kate went home after about half an hour, Edward had fallen asleep.[56]

Christmas Day, according to Edward, went off 'better than usual'. Ruth did not stay at George Street the whole of the holiday but returned on Boxing Day, when the two of them apparently visited the Board Inn. Ruth was seen haranguing Edward nearby.

'Are you … coming?'

'If you don't I … kill you.'

'For God's sake,' he pleaded, 'come inside.'

They probably carried on arguing. But by the evening, Edward, not surprisingly, had a bad headache, and claimed, not terribly convincingly, that he did not know whether or not a bullet that Ruth had fired into a wall had been aimed at him.[57] The Christmas holiday, like so many periods in Edward and Ruth's relationship, saw them getting back together, separating, arguing and threatening one another. It was the last Christmas – indeed the last few days – that they were to spend together.

8

'I have shot a woman' [1]

THE WEATHER WORSENED over the next few days. It snowed heavily on the morning of Sunday 27 December, and the following day Wolverhampton Corporation hired 300 men to bolster the efforts of its existing workforce to clear the town of snow.[2] There was a further heavy snowfall the next day, and it remained 'bitterly cold'.[3] In fact, according to the *Daily Mail*, it was the coldest day for nearly thirty years.[4] The local press too made much of the severity of the weather. Indeed, the opening paragraph of the *Express and Star*'s story of what it called the 'Wolverhampton Tragedy' – Edward's shooting of Ruth – reads like a pastiche of Victorian and Edwardian melodrama.

> Everything seemed to give the lie to the barest suggestion of tragedy. Clean snow lay in deep drifts on roadway and pavement. It crowned the ivy which clings to these rather old-fashioned houses; it made the heavy iron fences around them look vague and indefinite, while whitened portico and gables increased the picturesqueness of the scene. Complete silence prevailed, and in the fine square beyond stood the historic church of St John, its imposing outline touched into further glory by Nature, the great artist. Yet there was tragedy. It had been enacted there. The grim monster is fond of contrasts like this. In the solemn hush of this street, the residence of several doctors, and one of the most interesting residential quarters of Wolverhampton, death had reaped a harvest. The scene of the shocking affair was No. 2, George-street.[5]

'Under the influence' [6]

The bad weather meant that neither Edward nor Ruth left the house much in the days following the Christmas holiday. But when they did, they seemed unable to avoid drawing attention to themselves. Ruth was drinking again and there is a story, though it may be apocryphal, that she and Edward had an argument at the Board Inn early on 29 December (the day that Edward went on to shoot her). According to this version of events, Ruth objected to Edward buying a round of drinks. Determined, presumably, to show those in the pub that he was able to afford it, Edward gave her a £5 note. Determined, presumably, to show them that she could not be bought or patronised, Ruth dropped the note onto the stove.[7]

Whether or not this story is true, we know what happened later in the day. Edward decided that he needed domestic help, so during the early afternoon, Ruth went to the home of Kate Maddox, the fifteen-year-old whom Edward had employed 'to mind baby and run errands', until she and the other servants walked out just before Christmas.[8] On her way to Kate's house, Ruth bumped into an acquaintance, Alice Finley. They got talking, Ruth remarking that she would be late getting Edward's dinner, Alice urging her to hurry up 'and not have a bother'.

'I intend neither being a man or a mouse,' Ruth retorted. 'I am not going to let him put other women before me. I intend doing him in myself, and someone else.'

'Don't say that,' warned Finley, 'or they will put you in prison.'[9]

Ruth reached Kate's house at about half past three. The teenager had probably not met Ruth before, and she felt her visitor to be 'under the influence' – 'not sober and not drunk', as she put it later. However, she must have known who Ruth was because she agreed to return with her to work for Edward, this time as a general servant.[10] Ruth was anxious to get back as quickly as possible to make Edward his tea, so she and Kate ran part of the way, arriving at George Street at about four o'clock.[11]

When they got there, Ruth let them in through the front door. Seeing that the floors were clean but that the beds had not been made, Ruth saw to the beds, and together they cleaned the kitchen, the middle room and the drawing room, Ruth sweeping while Kate whitened the hearth. After they had been in the house for about an hour, Ruth poured herself a large tumbler of whisky and water – more whisky than water – from a large stone whisky bottle. About an hour later, she had a second glass, and not long afterwards a third. Her face became redder, recalled Kate, 'but she did not seem to stagger'.[12]

There were two visitors to the house. At about 7.30, Kate heard somebody knocking at the front door, and Ruth came downstairs to answer it. There were sounds of a man's voice, and whoever it was left, and Ruth went back upstairs.[13] Shortly afterwards, at about a quarter to eight, Kate heard another knock at the front door and this time she recognised Edward Lawrence's voice.

There were the makings of another combustible situation. Ruth had been drinking earlier in the day, and had drunk three glasses of whisky since returning to the house. In fact, Kate believed that by the time Edward arrived home, Ruth was 'under the influence' – she could smell the drink on her breath. Edward had also been drinking, in his case at the Board Inn. But it is not clear how much he had drunk or what impact it had on him. On the one hand, those who were with him in the pub insisted that they saw nothing to suggest that anything had 'ruffled his feeling'. Indeed, according to someone who arrived just as he was leaving, he 'looked as jolly as ever'.[14] On the other hand, Kate Maddox believed that when he got back to George Street, he was 'under the influence of drink'. Although she had only worked for Edward for a few weeks, she could tell, she said, when he was in this state.[15]

The volatility of the situation was compounded by the fact that, as Ruth had feared, the dinner was not ready when Edward arrived home. Although she had helped Kate by peeling the potatoes and preparing the brussel sprouts, they had not managed to get everything finished in time.[16] Edward came into the kitchen.

'Hello Kate have you come back again?'

'Yes sir.'[17]

He sent her upstairs to ask Ruth where the whisky bottle was. Ruth was doing her hair, but came downstairs after a few minutes and asked him which bottle he meant. 'The big one,' he explained. Kate could not find it and went upstairs again to speak to Ruth, who told her that it was in the pantry. Edward then called Kate to join him in the sitting room, where he made a desultory attempt to proposition her. He put his arm round her neck and tried to kiss her. But she would not let him.[18] Perhaps such advances were part and parcel of working for Edward; in all events Kate did not seem either unduly surprised or upset by Edward's advances.

Kate returned to the kitchen, while Edward took the whisky bottle from the pantry into the sitting room. Shortly afterwards, Ruth came downstairs, and Edward asked her who it was that had emptied the bottle.

'Not me,' she replied.[19]

Edward poured himself a whisky and water, and turning to Ruth, accused her two or three times of being drunk. She, in turn, denied it two or three times (without, Kate remarked, flying into a temper). Ruth then called Kate into the kitchen, and asked her whether or not she thought she was drunk.

This, of course, put the young girl in a difficult position. Although – or perhaps because – she had seen Ruth drink three glasses of whisky and water (and Edward a glass of whisky), she replied that she did not think so. This only aggravated Edward, who ordered Ruth to leave the house. She began to do as she was told, taking off her slippers and putting on her outdoor boots.

'Now go out of my house,' Edward repeated.

'Give me my week's wages.'

It was an argument they had rehearsed many times before.

'I haven't got any,' he said, standing up and taking a step towards her. 'Now go out of my house when I tell you.'[20]

Ruth's response was to pick up a cruet stand and a couple of beer glasses from the table that she and Kate had laid for dinner. When Edward asked her what she was going to do with them, she replied, 'I'll soon show you if you start.'[21] He sat down, and she put them back on the table. It was now about ten to nine, and Ruth told Kate to collect her clothes. When she had done so, Ruth let the girl out by the front door, seeing her off with the words, 'Go straight home.' As Kate left, the last thing she saw was Ruth fastening the door behind her. 'When I left,' Kate recalled, 'there was no one else but Prisoner and Miss Hadley.'[22]

'She is not dead, is she?'[23]

It would be difficult to exaggerate the significance – or the tragedy – of what happened next. Within the next hour, Ruth was shot in the head. Within the next few hours she was dead, the cause of death 'murder'.[24]

The press reported the case, the police investigated it, and the criminal justice system worked its way towards a resolution. But there is a black hole at the core of events. We shall never know for sure what took place between Edward Lawrence and Ruth Hadley after their young servant left them on the evening of 29 December 1908. What happened next remains today, as it was a hundred years ago, unknown – and unknowable – to all but the two people who were in the house at the time of the shooting. And of course, only one of them was alive to give his version of events. We have to rely therefore upon a combination of Edward's claims (however self-serving), the forensic evidence (however unsatisfactory), and our own skills of imagination and reconstruction (however restricted).

What we do know is that Ruth sent Kate home at about ten to nine. We also know that at about the same time, Edward's and Ruth's next-door neighbours (at number 3), the Boultons, were returning to their house. The front doors of numbers 2 and 3 George Street were immediately opposite one another, inside a covered passage separating the two houses, and as they turned up the passage towards their front door, the Boultons heard what they described as 'something go off'.

'What is that?' Joseph Boulton said to his wife.

'It's another door banging, I suppose,' she replied.[25]

But what they heard next probably confirmed what they already knew, or suspected, about their neighbour's behaviour. They could make out Edward, inside 2 George Street, talking, apparently to himself:

'Where is the key to this bloody door?'

'I'm going to fetch some one in.'[26]

Almost immediately after Mr and Mrs Boulton heard 'something go off', Lawrence's other neighbour (at number 1), Dr Thomas Galbraith,[27] went out to post a letter in the pillar box on the opposite side of the street. He left his front door open behind him, and while he was out Edward, who had unlocked his door 'at the top of the entry', ran into the street, went into Galbraith's surgery, and waited for him in the hall.

'Come with me, at once,' he urged the doctor. Lawrence was speaking, Galbraith recalled later, 'quite distinctly but low.'[28]

Dr Galbraith asked him what the matter was.

'Come at once. It is urgent: there is no time to lose.'

Again, Dr Galbraith asked him what the matter was.

'I have shot a woman.'[29]

Edward and the doctor set off together, and as they passed the front door of number 2, Edward explained that they would have to go in at the back:

'We cannot get in there as the woman has the key in her pocket.'

They continued up the passage, through the yard door, across the yard to the washhouse door, and into the washhouse. However, the doctor did not like the fact that Edward, whom he thought had been drinking, locked the yard door behind them and wanted to lock the washhouse door as well. Galbraith therefore took the precaution of putting the key in his pocket, so that he would be able to unlock the yard door and go back outside if he should need to look for assistance. When he did so, he saw another neighbour, Dr Carter, who lived at number 9, and he asked him to come back with him to the scene of the shooting.[30]

They too went along the passage between numbers 2 and 3, into the washhouse. When they reached the door that divided the washhouse from the kitchen, they met Edward, who urged them to be quick.[31]

'I have brought another doctor – Dr Carter,' said Galbraith.

The three of them went into the sitting room, where they found a young woman, whom they learned subsequently to be Ruth Hadley. She was wearing her outdoor clothes, and although her hat had fallen off, it was still fixed to her hair which, they noticed, was 'in a disordered condition'.[32] According to Dr Galbraith's subsequent statement, Ruth was

> lying on her back on the floor with her head towards the window and slightly towards the kitchen door … The body and legs were between the table and the sideboard. I examined the body and found a round wound on the right temple from which blood and brain-substance was exuding … She was deeply unconscious and was breathing heavily …[33]

There were signs of a struggle. On the table there was a side dish, with meat on it, that had one of its edges broken. There was a drawer that had been pulled out of the sideboard and its contents scattered about. There were knives under the front of the drawer, and on the floor there was broken crockery, including some lying underneath the injured woman's leg and body. Also on the floor, between the table and the sideboard, were two pairs of tongs, a black pair at Ruth's feet and a brass pair about a metre away, towards the drawing room. In fact, when Edward spoke next, he seemed to be pointing to the tongs and the broken crockery rather than to his injured lover:

'For God's sake do what you can for her. Be quick. Be quick. She is not dead, is she?'[34]

According to the doctors, Edward then went on to make a series of what seemed to be highly incriminating remarks. But although Galbraith and Carter must have realised that their evidence as to Edward's demeanour – what he said, and how he said it – was likely to be of considerable importance in any future legal proceedings, they were not as careful as they might have been. Carter admitted later that he made his notes as to what happened 'not at the moment but next day'; and that he and Dr Galbraith then compared their notes, and found that they were in agreement.[35] To the best of our knowledge, this is what Edward said as the two doctors went about their business.

'I did it in self-defence.'

'I am glad I've done it.'

'You do not know what a bad woman she is; and what a life she has led me during the last two months.'[36]

The doctors did what they could for Ruth, and then went next door to Dr Galbraith's house in order to collect dressings and bandages. While they were there, they telephoned both the police station and the general hospital, before returning to dress the injured woman's head. As they did so, Lawrence, they recalled, was marching up and down the room 'in a state of great excitement', and kept repeating, 'I did it in self-defence.'[37] According to Dr Carter, he 'was not exactly drunk'. Nonetheless, 'He was excited. He had certainly had some drink.'[38]

'She had shot herself'[39]

Dr Galbraith's phone call reached Wolverhampton's main police station at ten o'clock, and two of the force's most senior officers, inspector William Hill and inspector George Haynes, set off for George Street.[40] They would not have been used to dealing with cases such as this. The second half of the nineteenth century had seen a sustained decline in crimes of violence against the person, so that by the early years of the twentieth century the homicide rate stood at just ten per million of the population. As the criminal registrar noted contentedly in 1908, the previous fifty years had witnessed an 'enormous diminution of assaults ... a gratifying improvement reflecting the general amelioration of manners'.[41]

Moreover, the Victorian and Edwardian police were inclined to look kindly on the middle class. This was a time, it must be remembered, before the growth of motoring, and to a lesser extent recreational drug-taking, transformed the relationship between the police, the middle class and the working class.[42] 'It was universally understood,' claims F.M.L. Thompson, 'that gentlemanly drunks were not to be molested, although they might be helped home or into a cab.'[43]

Nevertheless, it would be difficult for the two officers to approach the case in an open or generous frame of mind. Inspector Hill, for one, had come across Edward before: 'I have known Lawrence some years and continually have seen him at nights under the influence of drink.'[44] Whatever Hill and Haynes talked about as they responded to the doctors' call, it did not take them long to travel the short distance from the police station to George Street. When they arrived, they knocked on the front door and, getting no reply, tried again before going round to the rear of the house. Entering the building through the back kitchen, they found Edward standing in the sitting room/middle room with his back to the fire and his hands in his trouser pockets.

It did not take the officers long to decide what they thought had happened. They could see a woman lying on her back near the window. They concluded that two bullets had been fired: the woman had a bullet wound on the right side of her head, and there were signs of another bullet having gone through both the window and the window blind. The injured woman was unconscious but still breathing, with blood flowing from her head, and more blood on the floor where she was lying. The policemen found some 'broken things', which they collected up. They then began their questioning.

It might have been shock; it might have been guilt; or it may have been the drink. No doubt, it was a combination of all three, but Edward's responses were scarcely calculated to help his cause.

'Who's this?' asked inspector Hill.

'It's a woman I should think,' Edward replied.

'Who's done this?'

'I don't know.'[45]

The policemen did not seal off the crime scene. 'Later on,' recalled next-door-neighbour Joseph Boulton, 'I went into the house, and I saw the woman lying underneath the window in the middle room. Her head was bandaged and the doctors had gone. Lawrence was there, and so were the police.'[46] Meanwhile, inspector Hill explained to Edward the serious situation in which he now found himself:

'I'm going to arrest you on a serious charge, and anything you say may be used in evidence against you.'

He then charged Edward with shooting Ruth Hadley with a revolver, with intent to murder her. Edward did not reply.[47]

While inspector Hill was questioning Edward, his colleague noticed something glinting in his right-hand coat pocket.

'I've got it,' exclaimed Haynes, removing a revolver from Edward's pocket, and putting it into his own pocket.

'You've got my revolver,' protested Edward.[48]

It was now twenty past ten. Inspector Haynes took charge of Edward,[49] and inspector Hill, it seems, went outside to meet the ambulance which had just arrived from the hospital. This left Haynes and the accused alone together in the house.

'What am I charged with?' asked Edward.

'Inspector Hill has just told you,' Haynes replied, and repeated the charge.

According to Haynes, Edward then made the following statement.

I took the revolver out of her hand as soon as she had shot herself,
and put it in my pocket. I knew bloody well she would shoot herself.
She only put it to her head like this [putting his hand to his temple].

And pulled the thing. She has had the revolver in her possession for two days. I have been abroad, as you know and have always been in the habit of having it under my pillow.[50]

The porter who had accompanied the ambulance from the general hospital came into the house. By this time, he reported later, there were three policemen in the building, and Ruth was still alive. Doctors Carter and Galbraith were also still there, and together they helped the police to get Ruth onto a stretcher and into the ambulance, which the porter drove the short distance to the hospital.[51] However, despite the staff's efforts at artificial respiration, Ruth died at 11.35 p.m.[52]

An operating theatre in Wolverhampton General Hospital, where Ruth Hadley was taken after Edward Lawrence shot her in December 1908.

BY COURTESY OF WOLVERHAMPTON ARCHIVES

9

'The gravity of his position'[1]

EVEN SOMEONE as resilient and self-regarding as Edward must have found the hours, days and weeks following Ruth's shooting disturbing and disorientating. Nothing, presumably, could ever prepare a privately educated, prosperous businessman for the trauma of being taken into police custody, charged with murder and put on trial in front of family, friends and acquaintances, not to mention a prurient press and a voracious reading public. Edward had to cope not only with the shock of being arrested, but with then being told almost immediately that Ruth had died. He had to learn to adjust to the demands of the criminal justice system, as well as finding a way of coping with the physical and psychological pressures of not being allowed to drink. His humiliation, both private and public, seemed at once well-nigh complete and well-nigh irredeemable.

'A voluntary statement'[2]

Edward, of course, was no legal innocent. He and Ruth were known to the police, and he had been badly bruised in the unsuccessful and embarrassing court cases he had brought against Lottie Davies and the clerk from his brewery. But he must have been totally unprepared for what happening to him now. As soon as inspectors Hill and Haynes had helped to put Ruth into the ambulance at George Street, they took Edward by cab the short distance to Wolverhampton's main police station.[3] Their prisoner, according to inspector Hill, was 'sensible, but he had had some liquor. I should say that he knew what he was doing.'[4] Hill cautioned Edward and charged him with feloniously wounding Ruth Hadley by shooting her in the head with a revolver with intent to murder her.

'To murder her?' retorted Edward. 'That's all right.'[5]

He learned soon enough that Ruth had died from her injuries. Shortly before midnight, he sent for inspector Haynes saying that he wished to make a statement. Haynes went with Hill to see Edward in his cell, where he confirmed that he wanted to explain what had happened at George Street. Haynes stressed that he would be doing so on a voluntary basis, and Hill then cautioned him, before adding abruptly, 'I must also tell you that the woman Ruth Hadley is dead.'[6]

Although Edward was drowsy and had still to sober up,[7] it seems that the news of Ruth's death knocked any remaining bravado out of him. Some time later, he spoke again to the two inspectors, along with a sergeant Martin who had formal charge of him.

'Have I to make a statement before you three?'

Haynes replied that if he wished to make such a statement, they would make a note of it.

'All right I will.'[8]

He did so, and Haynes, kneeling by a chair, wrote down what he said.

Police Cells,
December 30th, 1908

I Edward Lawrence wish to make a voluntary statement, + I make the following statement to Inspector Haynes:

The woman has lived with me (But not in my house altogether) for years + I wanted her to go + by arrangement she was going, she stole my revolver from under the pillow. I always kept one there ever since I had a house, ever since she lived with [me], I have travelled abroad + and I always kept a revolver near me + I done the same thing here, under my pillow always, Two days ago she took it + I have never seen it since [until I picked it up from my floor I put it in my pocket, and you took] it out. I did not think she was hurt I have asked her where it was + she said she had put it away. Twenty times she has told me she would either shoot herself or me.[9]

Haynes read the statement back to Edward, and asked him to sign it. Edward read it, made some minor modifications, and crossed out the words, 'until I picked it up from my floor I put it in my pocket and you took'. But still he refused to sign the draft that had been put before him.[10] The officers then left Edward to rest and sober up in his cell for what was left of the night.

'The barrell was foul'[11]

Meanwhile, the two policemen continued with their enquiries. Inspector Haynes checked Edward's gun, which he identified as a .383 calibre weapon (sometimes known as a 'brute revolver' because of its size and the difficulty of handling it).[12] He discovered five cartridges (four live, and one spent), and saw too that one of the chambers had recently been discharged: 'the barrell,' he reported, 'was foul.'[13] The fact that there was one empty chamber but that (as they later discovered) two bullets had been fired, suggested, they concluded, that Edward had reloaded the gun in an attempt to conceal the fact that he had shot Ruth twice. (If the detectives were right in their supposition, it meant of course that the shooting was unlikely to have been an accident.[14])

Then, at about three o'clock in the morning, inspectors Hill and Haynes returned to George Street. When they went into the front bedroom on the first floor, they found it 'in a state of confusion'. Bedding, including the mattress, was lying on the floor at the foot of the bed, and there were books, papers and magazines scattered around the room. In the right-hand drawer of the washstand, Haynes discovered a second revolver, a small box containing six cartridges and another containing forty-six. Comparing them with those found on their prisoner, he discovered that they were similar in make and size, that they fitted Edward's revolver, and that the other six cartridges fitted the weapon found in the washstand.[15]

Hill and Haynes went downstairs into the front room, the latter spotting a hole in the window blind, and another in the window immediately behind it. Following what he took to be the flight of a bullet, he discovered a mark on the lobby window overlooking the yard, showing where, he supposed, the bullet had glanced off an outer fence and then off a wall.[16] In the front room itself, he found the bars of the grate lying on the hearth, and what he described as a broken 'fancy flower pot' lying on the floor.[17]

Haynes made a further examination of the middle sitting room, compiling a list of what he saw: a couch, a sideboard, an easy chair and four small chairs, a bundle of pictures against the end of the sideboard, and another bundle on a chair near the window. On the floor was the left-hand drawer of the sideboard, with what seemed to be its contents strewn about. He noticed too that there was broken crockery, cooked potatoes, spoons, forks, a carving knife and fork, and two pairs of tongs. The table was laid for supper, though with several broken plates, and a dish with a broken edge containing stewed meat.[18]

There were also a number of legal/medical matters for the authorities to attend to. Ruth's sister, Kate Lewis (who had last seen her on Christmas Eve), identified the dead woman's body in the mortuary.[19] The house surgeon at the general hospital, Dr Powell, then conducted a post mortem examination, in the presence of several of his colleagues including one of the hospital's honorary surgeons.[20] Powell had been present when Ruth was undressed, and he noticed that there was a tear in the sleeve of her blouse. She was, he observed, 'a well-nourished woman'.[21]

The house surgeon found three sets of injuries on Ruth's body. There were two bruises on the back of her left wrist, a scratch on the third finger of her left hand and several small bruises on her left arm. There were also two holes below her right shoulder: one was circular, half an inch across; the other 'crescented in shape', half an inch long and a quarter of an inch wide. Finally, on her temple, Powell noticed a wound with a 'track' leading backwards to a hole in the skull in front of her ear. Although there was no evidence of blackening round the wound or 'on the clothing of the right shoulder', Dr Powell discovered that, 'In the posterior end of this fracture a small piece of lead was embedded.' In all, he found eleven pieces of lead, weighing 43 grains.[22]

Powell was convinced not only that the cause of Ruth's death was the bullet wound below her shoulder but that it could not possibly have been self-inflicted. He did not think it possible for somebody holding a revolver in her right hand to cause such a wound in her right shoulder by pulling the trigger with her forefinger (although she might have been able to do so, he conceded later, by using her thumb). He also believed that the absence of singeing around the wound meant that the revolver had been held some distance from the body.[23]

'The capital offence'[24]

There were a number of further developments when Edward awoke – or was woken – in his cell the following morning (30 December). His estranged wife, Margaret, called to see him. So too, presumably, did his solicitor, Mr Copeland, who was to represent him at the police court later in the day. Inspectors Hill and Haynes certainly saw him, because they needed to change the charge against him from one of attempted murder to one of murder. Accordingly, at ten o'clock, Hill cautioned Edward, before charging him formally, 'with having at Wolverhampton on the 29th December 1908 feloniously wilfully and of his malice aforethought did kill and murder one Ruth Hadley.'

'Well there is one thing I did not do it,' replied Edward, before adding, rather unhelpfully, 'You were not there when it was done.'[25]

Despite the fact that Edward, like all those charged, was considered innocent until proven guilty, the criminal justice system did nothing at all to protect his reputation or his standing in the community. Time after time over the next few weeks, the legal process stripped him of virtually all remaining shreds of dignity and respectability, laying bare his humiliation for readers of the local press to enjoy, condemn or gloat over according to taste.

Later the same morning, Edward made the first of his many court appearances. This entailed being taken the short distance from the police station to the cells in the basement underneath the town hall. News had begun to spread both about Ruth's death and about the fact that Edward was to appear in the town's police court. Despite the bad weather, small groups of men stood around the town hall discussing the case. When the door of the court was opened just before eleven o'clock, there was a rush for seats, and the room was soon full. However, at eleven o'clock, the stipendiary magistrate's clerk announced that no cases would be taken until midday because the stipendiary, Mr Neville, had been delayed by the adverse weather. Many of the spectators left the building, but a number remained until the police constable on duty suggested that the court should be cleared.[26]

The court reconvened at a quarter to twelve, when there was 'just as eager a demand for seats'. Half an hour later, the stipendiary magistrate arrived, and after the disposal of one minor case, the chief constable of Wolverhampton, Captain Burnett, called the prisoner: 'Edward Lawrence.'

Edward walked slowly up the steps from the cells, wearing a dark overcoat, his face, it was reported, 'exceptionally flushed'.

'You are charged,' confirmed the magistrate's clerk, 'that at Wolverhampton yesterday you did feloniously, wilfully, and of your malice aforethought kill and murder one Ruth Hadley.'[27]

The chief constable explained that the prisoner had originally been charged with attempted murder, but that this charge would be dropped now that the woman had died from her injuries. He explained, too, that he had consulted the borough coroner, who would open an inquest the following day. All that he proposed to do at this sitting was to call inspector Hill, who would provide sufficient evidence, he believed, to justify remanding Edward in custody for a week. This he did, examining Hill, who explained how he and his colleague, inspector Haynes, had gone to George Street the previous evening. He reported that they had found Ruth Hadley injured, had questioned Lawrence, had discovered the revolver upon his person, and gone on to charge him 'with the capital offence'.

Asked by the stipendiary magistrate if he had anything to say, Lawrence replied, 'Yes, sir.'

'No, no,' interjected Mr Copeland, telling the stipendiary that he was representing the accused.

Edward was remanded for a week, and taken back to the cells. He must have found this highly disturbing: the other six occupants of the cells were charged with everything from wilful murder to unlawfully pawning a man's jacket.[28]

Later in the day, the police surgeon informed the chief constable that Edward was 'suffering from palpitation' ('bordering on a state of delirium tremens' according to Inspector Haynes),[29] and it was decided that he should be transferred to HM Prison, Stafford, where he could receive 'special medical attention'.[30] He was moved there just after half past two. Handcuffed to one police officer and accompanied by another, he was driven by cab to Wolverhampton railway station. Wearing a billycock hat and 'a stylishly cut dark grey coat', he was the centre of attention as he and his entourage travelled the short distance through the centre of the town to catch the train.[31]

Stafford Prison, like all late nineteenth- and early twentieth-century penal institutions, was an intimidating place. Enlarged until it occupied an area of seven acres, it was supposedly capable of accommodating over 800 prisoners, although its usual complement was fewer than half that number, and when Edward was admitted there were 563 men and 42 women in custody.[32] When Edward arrived, he was given prison clothes, taken to the hospital and placed under special observation. Indeed, it was claimed later that 'on account of his condition', a padded cell had been prepared for him.[33] Whether or not this was true, it is certainly the case that by the turn of the century prison doctors had begun to pay particular attention to remand prisoners whose mental condition was giving magistrates cause for concern.[34]

In due course, therefore, Stafford's medical officer, Dr Mander, wrote a detailed report for the prison governor on the condition of their new, high-profile inmate.[35] Mander concluded that none of Edward's physical injuries was serious: he had slight bruising and tenderness under his left eye, and small bruises on his back, right shin, left hand, right and left forearms, and left elbow (the result perhaps of a struggle). The latter was 'the most severe and of a purple colour in the centre shading to yellow at the edges'.

Edward's other symptoms were more worrying: his tongue was 'flabby and indented, coated with a thick fur and very tremulous; his hand and arms were tremulous, the heart's action quick and feeble'. Dr Mander's diagnosis was unequivocal: 'His general aspect and bearing suggested that he was a very heavy drinker and had recently been indulging very freely.'[36] He was short-tempered and unsure of the day and the date.

> Mentally he was irritable, was inclined to resent being questioned and did not realize the gravity of his position, treating the charge against him as a preposterous one. There was also some mental confusion as to time, the prisoner stating that he had had nothing to drink for two days as he had been in custody, whereas he had only been arrested the day before. When asked the day of the week he said it was Friday and was not sure whether it was the 30th or 31st [It was Wednesday the 30th].[37]

Edward would have been more irritable and resentful still if he had known what was being written about him in the local press.[38] The *Express and Star*'s account of the 'Wolverhampton Tragedy' moved more or less seamlessly from the atmospheric evocation of George Street cited in the previous chapter, to a detailed and carefully neutral account of the events of the previous twenty-four hours, to an innuendo-laden assault on Edward's character and behaviour. It began with the break-up of his marriage.

> Edward Lawrence is one of the best-known men in Wolverhampton … The accused man married a West Bromwich lady, by whom he has a large family. The domestic life of Edward Lawrence and his wife was not a happy one, and the parties separated some three or four years ago.

The report moved on to the circles that Edward moved in, his liking for drinking and his interest in gambling.

> Lawrence had many friends … among this class the news of the sensational incident has created some consternation. To them, Teddy, as they familiarly called him, was 'a brick' and they would have nothing said against him. A man of medium and sturdy stature, with a face always ruddy and eyes glistening, and a moustache of a dark brown colour, Lawrence was easily recognizable. He has been what might be described as a 'pal' to a good number of men; for with a certain section he was generous and good-natured, and they will miss

him from his favourite haunts. He took a keen interest in horse-racing, and if it was possible for him to do anybody a good turn in that direction he would do it.[39]

'Very weak, nervous and trembling'[40]

Gradually, as one would expect, Edward began to sober up. But it is not clear how quickly or how completely his recovery took place. According to the prison's medical officer, Dr Mander, Edward's 'mental condition soon improved, and in a day or two his mind became clearer, and he appeared to realise the gravity of his position, and was able to make arrangements with his solicitor for his defence.'[41] Others were less optimistic. Four days after his arrest, Edward received a visit from another medical man, Dr Bankier,[42] a Wolverhampton practitioner whom Edward's solicitor had engaged to assess his condition. Bankier's report confirmed that physically there was little seriously wrong with Edward. He too found several minor injuries, including bruises on his right arm and left shin, a swelling on his left temple, a bruise and tenderness under his left eyelid, and several bruises on his left arm. The bruise he discovered on Lawrence's left elbow, he conceded, was 'severe ... and might have been caused within four days'.[43]

However, Dr Bankier's view as to the other aspects of Edward's medical condition was, like Mander's, far less sanguine. He reported that Edward was still 'very weak nervous and trembling'. 'He had a very congested face – eyes much inflamed and the tongue covered with thick creamy fur – He was suffering very much from thirst ... His pulse was very weak.' The signs, he believed, were inescapable: 'he had the appearance of a man recovering from an attack of delirium tremens and he was in my opinion in such a condition that he might at any moment have an attack of that disease.'[44]

It is no great surprise therefore that Edward did not attend the coroner's inquest into Ruth's death: perhaps he was too ill, or perhaps his solicitor wanted him out of the way so as to avoid the possibility of any further outbursts. In fact, there were only a few people in the sessions court when the borough coroner, Mr Wilcock, opened the enquiry into Ruth's death. However, those who were present included the chief constable, Edward's solicitor Copeland, and Smith Dorsett of Birmingham whom Copeland had instructed in the case.[45] The jury was sworn in, and two witnesses gave evidence.

Ruth's sister, Kate Lewis, confirmed the nature of the dead woman's relationship with Edward.

'Where had she lately been living?' asked the coroner.

'At No. 2, George-street.'

'For how long to your knowledge?'

'Since Christmas Eve.'

'Did she go there on that date?'

'I cannot say; that was the last time I saw her alive.'

'Was she at that time to your knowledge living with Edward Lawrence?'

'Yes.'

'How long had she cohabited with him?'

'About five years.'

Kate finished her evidence by confirming that Edward and Ruth had kept a servant – and fatally, one would think, for both their reputations, that they had had a child together.[46]

Indeed, Edward's counsel, Smith Dorsett, went on to confirm that damage had already been done – beyond the courts – to his client's reputation. The coroner was about to adjourn the inquest (so that copies of the depositions could be furnished to the defence team and the 'responsible authorities'), when Smith Dorsett intervened. Explaining that although he personally had every confidence in the press, he needed, he said, to alert the court to the 'unintentional mischief' that the newspapers' reporting might do. But it was not the *Express and Star* he had in his sights. His claim was that another paper that 'circulated in the town' had carried the headline, 'Murder in George-street: Brewer Arrested'. He feared that this 'sensational heading', with its assumption of guilt, 'would probably come to the ears of the gentlemen who would have to adjudicate in the case'. Serious as was the charge against his client, Smith Dorsett concluded, 'we have a complete answer to this enquiry'.

'Perhaps you had better not say any more,' the coroner advised Smith Dorsett. 'I have not the slightest doubt that your remarks will bring about all you desire.'

He then adjourned the enquiry for a week.[47]

Meanwhile, the police continued building their case. On the morning of 31 December, inspector Haynes accompanied local photographer Arthur Clark to George Street.[48] When they arrived, Clark took a number of photographs: one of the ground floor, middle room, which was still 'in great disorder';[49] and two from the yard, one of the window to the cloak room, the other of the window to the passage.[50] Haynes resumed the search of the yard and the sitting room. Near the sitting-room door, he discovered a bullet, with a small piece of wood attached to it;[51] near the sideboard, he unearthed an empty cartridge case with the same maker's name and mark as those on the cartridge taken from Edward's revolver. The bullet smelt of powder, he said, and seemed to have been used quite recently.[52] Later in the day, Haynes handed over to the chief constable one of the forty-six cartridges he had found in the box in the washstand.[53]

As Edward continued his recovery to something approaching full health, he was presumably kept informed by his solicitor, Copeland, about the progress both of the police investigation and of the defence team's efforts on his behalf. However, there was little that anyone could do to complete his recovery, to allay all his fears – or to persuade his sons to visit him in prison.[54] The three months between Edward's arrest and the start of his trial must have consisted of interminable periods of boredom and anxiety, interspersed with consultations with his professional advisers and visits to Wolverhampton for appearances before the coroner and the stipendiary magistrate.[55]

'Glanced keenly round the court'[56]

Edward was well enough – or was felt by his advisers to be well disciplined enough – to attend the adjourned inquest into Ruth's death which reopened at Wolverhampton town hall on 7 January. Although there was a fair attendance by members of the general public, surprisingly 'there did not appear to be any special interest manifested in the proceedings.'[57] The chief constable, Captain Burnett, was again present, and so too was Smith Dorsett who, instructed by Copeland, continued to watch proceedings on behalf of their client. Then shortly after the coroner took his seat, Drs Carter and Galbraith arrived.[58]

'Is Mr Lawrence present?' asked the coroner.

Edward entered the court and took a seat behind his legal team. He seemed to be in much better command of himself. 'He was smartly dressed in a light brown suit,' reported the *Midland Counties Express*, 'and glanced keenly round the court while the formalities were being carried through.'[59]

The coroner ordered Ruth's sister, Kate Lewis, to be recalled. She confirmed that the last time she had seen her sister alive was at 8.15 p.m. on Christmas Eve, when she had left George Street after helping Ruth to clean the house.[60] The next two witnesses provided evidence as to what happened at 2 George Street in the weeks leading up to Ruth's death. Both of them portrayed – perfectly truthfully but probably not very helpfully from Edward's point of view – a picture of a household run on lines far removed from conventional standards of propriety and respectability.

Elizabeth Wardle explained that she had begun working for Edward Lawrence as a general servant in the middle of December. At that time, she said, Lawrence was living with a Miss Stacey, whom he passed off as his wife. Shown a revolver by inspector Haynes, she told the coroner that Lawrence had kept it under his pillow in the bedroom he shared with Emma Stacey. She confirmed that she and Stacey had left the house on 22 December, but that she returned the following day to collect her slippers and pocket handkerchiefs. She took the opportunity, she added, to take Edward's – fully loaded – revolver from underneath his pillow. She took it, she went on, because, 'I noticed that Mr Lawrence seemed rather strange.'[61]

'What do you mean?' asked the coroner.

'He seemed rather excited. I knew the revolver was kept there, and from what a girl named Ethel Cross had told me ...'

At this point, members of the jury complained that they could not hear what was being said. Elizabeth tried again: 'I had noticed that Lawrence appeared excited when I first went into the house. In consequence of something that a girl named Ethel Cross had told me I was afraid, and took the revolver.'[62] During the course of these exchanges, those in court noticed, Edward made a number of notes, which he handed to his solicitor.[63]

The second witness was the fifteen-year-old servant, Kate Maddox. Giving evidence to such an enquiry would prove, one would have thought, a highly intimidating experience.[64] Perhaps she did not realise the importance of the occasion, or perhaps she was accustomed to being patronised by those in positions of authority. Whatever the reason, she did seem unduly overawed. Questioned by the coroner, she explained that she had been engaged by Miss Stacey 'to mind baby and to run errands', but that she, together with Emma Stacey, Ethel Cross and Elizabeth Wardle, had walked out on Edward on 22 December.

Her evidence confirmed the amount of drinking going on in the house. On the evening of Ruth's death, she recalled, Edward returned home at about a quarter to eight.

'What state was he in?' demanded the coroner.

'He was under the influence of drink, sir.'

'Why do you say that, my girl?'

'Because I can tell when he has had something to drink, sir.'

She went on to recount that Edward tried to kiss her, that Ruth too was 'under the influence of drink', and that the couple began to quarrel over whether or not Ruth was drunk, and in particular over whether or not she had drunk the whisky that Edward claimed to be missing.

'More whisky than water'[65]

Cross-examined by Smith Dorsett, Kate explained – not very helpfully for Edward – that when Emma Stacey had come downstairs crying and screaming three days before Christmas, Edward's response had been to threaten her with the gun he had in his trouser pocket: 'If you don't be quiet, I will quieten you for good.'

Kate went on to explain – more helpfully for Edward – that on the day of her death, Ruth had been drinking whisky and water as she cleaned the house.

'Was there more whisky than water,' asked Smith Dorsett. This provoked laughter – 'the first time,' remarked the *Midland Counties Express*, that anything had been said 'to stir the risibilities.'

'More whisky,' confirmed Kate.

She also confirmed that, when she left to go home, the house had been neat and tidy, with nothing out of place.

The next witness was Dr Galbraith, who told the court what happened when Lawrence called at his house, demanding that he go to see the injured woman. He explained that he returned with Edward, but went out again and found Dr Carter. Together, he said, they called the police and the hospital, did what they could for the injured woman, and helped to get her onto a stretcher and into the ambulance. He noticed what appeared to be signs of a struggle, and very clear indications that Edward 'had had something to drink'.

Dr Carter corroborated his colleague's evidence, adding that although Edward 'was not drunk, he was labouring under great excitement'. The coroner questioned the doctor closely – and leadingly – as to what Edward had said.

'Did he express pleasure or regret at having done it?'

'I think he said, "I did it in self-defence".'

'Did you make a note at the time?'

'No; but he constantly repeated, "I did it in self-defence".'

'Do you think he fully understood what he said?'

'I should say he did, but he was very distressed and excited.'[66]

It was the turn of the police to give evidence. Inspector Hill explained how he and inspector Haynes went to George Street in response to Dr Galbraith's telephone call. Once there, he charged Edward with attempted murder, took him to the police station, and then charged him formally with shooting Ruth Hadley.

'In what state did he appear to be?'

'He appeared to be sensible, but he had had some liquor. I should say he knew what he was doing.'[67]

Inspector Haynes was called next, and he corroborated Hill's evidence as to what they found when they went to George Street. The only new information he provided concerned the conversation he had with Edward while they were alone together after the charge of attempted murder had been put to him. Edward explained, he recalled, how it was that he came to have what seemed like the murder weapon in his possession. This, according to the policeman, was what he said:

> I took the revolver out of her hand as soon as she had shot herself, and put it in my pocket. I knew … well she would shoot herself. She only put it to her head like this (putting his hand to his temple), and pulled the thing. She has had the revolver in her possession for two days. I have been abroad as you know. I have always been in the habit of leaving it under my pillow.

Haynes went on to corroborate his colleague's evidence as to what happened once they reached the police station. He explained how Edward asked to make a statement, made it, but then refused to sign it. Haynes explained too that he examined the revolver and went through the rooms of George Street, which he found to be in some disarray. He finished his evidence by suggesting that if a pistol or a revolver filled with black powder was fired near to a person's face, two things would happen: it would discolour the face, and the wound would be surrounded by small, dark-coloured spots.

It had been a long session, and finally at ten past three the coroner adjourned 'for luncheon'.[68]

'On the resumption of the proceedings,' reported the *Midland Counties Express*, 'the court was crowded, and the evidence was listened to with the keenest possible interest.' When inspector Haynes resumed his evidence, the foreman of the jury asked him if he had found any bruises or injuries on Lawrence.

'No, sir; no visible marks; and he did not complain.'

Smith Dorsett saw an opportunity to undermine, or at least question, the credibility of police procedures.

'You did not examine him for bruises?'

'No, sir.'

'As a matter of fact, have you heard now he was bruised from his shoulder to his wrist?'

'This is the first time.'

'Was not a mark visible on his cheek?'

'There was an old mark on his cheek which I had seen previously.'

'Was there not an appearance of a new mark?'

'I did not see it.'

Smith Dorsett changed tack, the defence obviously intending to rely, in part at least, upon sacrificing Edward's character and reputation in order to try to save his life. (If it could be shown that Edward's heavy drinking and dissolute lifestyle had affected his capacity to function normally, it would be possible to argue that he had not known what he was doing on the night in question.) So when inspector Haynes told the court that Edward had been hurried away to Stafford after being remanded by the stipendiary magistrate, Smith Dorsett put it to him,

'Was this because he was on the verge of delirium tremens?'

'I believe so, sir.'

Haynes had gone too far. The chief constable intervened, pointing out that the doctor's certificate was to the effect that he was sent to Stafford because he was suffering from palpitations.

But Smith Dorsett was not easily deflected.

'Do you know that in consequence of that report the padded cell was prepared for him at Stafford?'

It was the coroner's turn to intervene: 'This officer could not say that.'

'Did you know he was put into prison clothes?' persisted Smith Dorsett.

Haynes knew now that he to be more circumspect.

'I don't know.'

'On account of his condition?'

'I don't know.'[69]

'Compression and laceration of the brain'[70]

The next witness was Dr Powell, the house surgeon at the general hospital who had performed the post mortem examination on Ruth. He told the court the results of his investigation, suggesting that the bruising on the dead woman's hand, wrist and arm might all have been caused by the artificial respiration attempted at the hospital. He went on to describe the two holes beneath her right shoulder, the hole in her temple, and the pieces of lead he had discovered in her skull.

'Was there any scorching of the skin of the arms or the head, or blackening of the clothing?' wondered the coroner.

'No,' Dr Powell replied; 'the head had been dressed before I saw it.'

The coroner did his best to establish whether more than one shot had been fired – and whether therefore the possibility of suicide (and accidental shooting) could be ruled out.

'From the position of the holes in the arm and in the clothing would the bullet have gone through them?'

'Yes.'

'The hole in the temple could that have been inflicted by the same shot or bullet that passed through the arm?'

'No.'

'In your opinion these injuries must have been caused by two bullets?'

'Yes.'

Dr Powell's evidence was almost at an end. But he made two further points. He doubted that the wounds to Ruth's body could have been self-inflicted; and he was in no doubt at all as to what it was that killed her: 'Death was caused by compression and laceration of the brain, due to a fracture of the skull, the result of a bullet, pieces of which were found embedded in the skull.'

Smith Dorsett then cross-examined Dr Powell with a view to undermining any impression that Edward might have been violent towards Ruth. This he did by getting the doctor to repeat that the bruises to Ruth's body might have been caused by the hospital's attempts at artificial respiration. He did so too by eliciting the doctor's agreement with the observation that, 'There was no evidence found on the body of the woman that she had ever been struck, or the subject of violence except the two wounds.'[71]

The coroner wondered whether Smith Dorsett intended to put Lawrence on the stand. 'I don't propose to call him,' Smith Dorsett replied, 'but I propose to call one witness, having regard to the question by the foreman of the jury' (as to whether there were any bruises or injuries on Lawrence).

Dr Bankier then entered the witness box, and explained that at the request of Edward's solicitor Mr Copeland, he had gone to Stafford Prison and examined the prisoner. He repeated what he said in his report, that in his view Edward seemed to be recovering from an attack of delirium tremens. He repeated too that Edward had bruising under his left eyelid, on his right arm and on the inside of his right shin.

'In your judgement,' asked Smith Dorsett, 'might these recent bruises have been inflicted four days before?'

'Yes.'

'Were they slight or severe?'

'The one on the elbow was distinctly severe,' replied Dr Powell.

'How might they have been caused?'

'By being pushed up against something or something thrown at him, such as a pair of tongs, or something of that sort.'

'Can you tell from his condition when you saw him in prison how he must have been some days before?'

'He must have been verging on delirium tremens.'

Dr Powell added, in answer to the coroner, that when an 'habitual drinker' such as Edward suddenly stopped drinking, it would have the tendency to bring on such a condition.

In his summing up, the coroner reviewed at some length the evidence that had been given. His guidance could scarcely have been clearer. He had no doubt, he said, that two shots had been fired; he had no doubt either that if the jury believed Edward Lawrence had fired them, nothing had been disclosed during the hearing that could justify his action. The question of Edward's physical and psychological condition, he stressed, was a matter for a higher court to deal with. Nonetheless, he made it obvious that in his view, there was no evidence to suggest that 'Lawrence had been injured, assaulted, or so provoked as to lose his judgement ...' If the jury believed the evidence, the coroner concluded, it was a case of murder.

The jury returned after an absence of less than twenty minutes. It was not a good sign. Their verdict was 'Wilful murder', and Edward was committed for trial on the coroner's warrant at Stafford Assizes.[72]

'I am glad I have done it'[73]

There seemed no end to Edward's humiliation. The very next day, he was brought back to appear before the stipendiary magistrate – and to go back over much the same ground as before. The first witness called was the photographer Arthur Clark, who produced the three photographs he had taken of the 'murder' scene: one of the middle room on the ground floor of George Street, and two of windows overlooking the yard. Smith Dorsett, who was again representing Edward's interests, stressed that the room had been tidied:

'There is no broken crockery or any tongs shown on the floor: these things had been removed, I suppose?'

'I suppose so.'

'I may take it this room was in great disorder?'

'Yes, that was so.'

There was just one further witness, Edward's next-door neighbour, Mr Boulton, before the court adjourned for lunch at half past one.[74]

When it resumed half an hour later, it was Dr Galbraith's turn to give evidence. He described the state of George Street when he arrived there: there were knives and dishes on the floor and the 'whole room was in a state of confusion'. Edward himself was 'excited, worried and anxious'.

'Was it not apparent,' demanded Smith Dorsett, 'that he had been heavily drinking?'

'To a medical man his face would indicate that,' Galbraith declared confidently.

However, the doctor was less convincing when pressed as to what else had happened.

'Have you told us everything that was said?'

'I think so, to the best of my recollection. He was, however, talking the whole time, and it was impossible, unless one were a shorthand writer, to record all that he said. There was one thing prisoner said that I have not said before. Lawrence did say, "I am glad I have done it. She is best dead."'

'Why didn't you say it today?'

'Well, it is not a pleasant thing to say, sir.'

'But you were to tell us everything that took place. Did something that Dr Carter said yesterday remind you of it?'

'Yes, it did.'

'When Dr Carter had given his evidence you didn't volunteer to alter your own?'

'No, sir, I did not.'

'When did Lawrence make use of that phrase?'

'About the time he said, "I have done it in self-defence."'

'And you really mean to say he said that?'

'I do.'

'Did you make a note of the conversation?'

'Not at the time, but on the following day.'

The next witness was Dr Carter who, not surprisingly, corroborated Dr Galbraith's evidence. Under cross-examination he confirmed that although Edward Lawrence had not been helplessly drunk, he was a man, he thought, who drank constantly and drank heavily. According to Carter, the prisoner did not show any pleasure in 'having done it': the phrase seemed merely to represent what the doctor described as a passionate outburst and a loss of control.

Dr Carter was followed into the witness box by inspector Hill, who repeated the evidence he had given previously. Smith Dorsett cross-examined him with regard to Edward's behaviour at the police station, and in particular the statement he dictated to his colleague, Haynes.

'Do you know how many statements Lawrence made up and tore up before this one?'

'Not one to my knowledge.'

'When Lawrence read it over did he appear to be half asleep?'

'Yes, he did.'

'Drunk and drowsy?'

'I would not say he was drunk: but he had certainly had some liquor and he was drowsy.'

Smith Dorsett pressed on with his efforts to paint Edward as a hopeless, helpless drunk, and so unaware of and/or not responsible for his actions.

'You know Lawrence, and has he latterly been indulging heavily in drink?'

'Yes. I have seen him going home when I have been on night duty, and I should say he was frequently under the influence of drink.'

'And that has been his practice lately?'

'I should say it has.'

The final witness to give evidence was Dr Powell, the house surgeon at the general hospital. He began by repeating his view that there would have been singeing if the wound to Ruth's head had been caused by a gun fired from a very short distance away. Smith Dorsett did his best to get him to agree that Ruth, rather than Edward, might have pulled the trigger.

'The wound in the temple might very easily have been self-inflicted?'

'I don't think so.'

'The wound in the temple had been dressed. Would not that destroy the evidence of singeing?'

'No.'

'Are you prepared to say positively that the wound was not self-inflicted?'

'Not positively.'

'Supposing she had this revolver, which is a repeater, in her hand, and someone was trying to take it off her, would not these wounds be accounted for by it going off in the struggle?'

'I don't think so; but, as I have said before, I have had no practical experience.'[75]

This marked the end of the prosecution evidence. The stipendiary's clerk read out the eleven depositions (which had been taken from Ruth's sister, Edward's and Ruth's servants, Edward's neighbours, the photographer, the house surgeon at the hospital and the two police inspectors).[76] It must have taken some time, and while he was doing so, Edward held brief conversations with Copeland and Smith Dorsett. Otherwise, 'Lawrence, with his right arm leaning on the top of the dock, listened intently to the evidence.'[77]

When the clerk had finished reading the depositions, Edward was asked to stand up. He was formally charged and cautioned, and committed for trial at Stafford Assizes on the charge of wilful murder.[78]

'Do you wish to make any statement now?' asked the stipendiary magistrate.

'I have nothing to say, except ...' began Edward.

'No, no,' interrupted Copeland (as he had at the original hearing).

'Except,' persisted Edward, 'that I am not guilty.'

'Do you wish to call any witnesses?' demanded the stipendiary.

'No, sir.'

The witnesses were bound over to appear at the assizes, and Edward was taken down to the cells.[79]

A group of Wolverhampton Borough policemen pictured in about 1900, a few years before the force undertook its investigation of Edward Lawrence's shooting of Ruth Hadley.

10

'A very lucky man'[1]

T HE PHRASE 'the lull before the storm' might have been invented to describe the next two months of Edward's life. The seven or eight weeks he spent in jail between his committal for trial and his appearance at Stafford Assizes at the beginning of March must have seemed endless. It was a period, like that immediately following his arrest, marked by discomfort, boredom and anxiety, leavened only by contact with his jailers, consultations with his legal team and visits perhaps from friends and relatives (though not, it seems, his sons).[2] Bereaved, apprehensive, powerless – and now sober – the stresses piling upon him must have seemed intolerable.

'Shadow of the noose'[3]

When his trial eventually started, Edward faced, yet again, the indignity of having his personal life – and his calamitous fall from grace – paraded for all the world to see. There were detailed reports, as one would expect, in West Midland newspapers such as the *Birmingham Gazette and Express*,[4] the *Staffordshire Advertiser*[5] and the *Staffordshire Chronicle*,[6] as well as in Wolverhampton's *Express and Star*,[7] the *Midland Counties Express*[8] and *Wolverhampton Chronicle*.[9] The case was also covered, albeit much more briefly, in regional newspapers such as the *Cheshire Daily Echo*,[10] quasi-national papers such as the *Manchester Guardian*,[11] and in papers of record including *The Times*.[12] Moreover, in subsequent years, the more sensational aspects of the case were quarried by local historians,[13] its juridical implications picked over by those interested in the history of advocacy or the development of legal procedure.[14] Indeed, the case found its way into something approaching the popular/historical mainstream, when it received the ultimate late twentieth-century accolade of a reconstruction on prime-time television as part of the 1989 series, 'Shadow of the Noose'.[15]

'Wilful murder' [16]

The 1909 winter assizes for Staffordshire opened at the shire hall, Stafford, on 1 March. Proceedings began with a meeting of the grand jury, whose job it was to decide whether the most serious cases should proceed to trial.[17] In his charge to the jury, Mr Justice Jelf explained that although the calendar did not contain an unusual number of cases, there were three charges of wilful murder which would require their gravest consideration.[18] The first indictment was against Edward. The other two were against another Wolverhampton man, Edward Jones, who was charged with killing his wife, and against a Black Country foundryman Joseph Dainty who was accused of murdering his lover in a suicide pact.[19]

Judge Jelf outlined the case against Edward. He suggested that he and Ruth had been in the habit of quarrelling, and that she had been likely to retaliate if she felt threatened: 'she was ready to take part if anything did occur; at any rate, not to take blows without returning them.' He went on to set out the events of the evening of 29 December, between Edward coming home to George Street and Ruth dying at the general hospital. There were, Jelf concluded, three possibilities other than murder: self-defence, suicide or manslaughter. Self-defence could be ruled out: 'Whatever the confusion of the room, self-defence would seem to be impossible in the case of an unarmed woman.' Suicide could also be excluded: 'they would hear from the doctors that they did not think this could have been possible.' This left manslaughter.

> It might be said there was a struggle. All these things – the commotion upstairs and downstairs, the conduct of the woman in taking up the cruet, and the fact that she had been drinking might go to show that the thing was done in a struggle by a man who had been drinking. If this was so the charge might be reduced from murder to manslaughter. That was a matter, however, which the jury would not have to go into, and he thought they would find it their duty to return a true bill.

The proceedings continued, the judge moving on to the indictment against the other two accused. In due course the grand jury did as it was bid, returning true bills for 'Wilful Murder' against all three of the men before them. Edward's trial was fixed to begin two days later, Wednesday 3 March.[20]

'More recent periods of their intimacy'[21]

It is easy to see the appeal of Edward Lawrence's trial, whether to sensation seekers, local historians, legal scholars or drama/documentary film makers. A major part of its attraction lay in the fact that Edward's legal team (led by Copeland and Smith Dorsett) could afford to engage Edward Marshall Hall to represent their client.[22] The cost of mounting Edward's defence must have been enormous. Smith Dorsett, for instance, was very well thought of. 'We were taken "special",' recalled his clerk, 'which meant a fifty-guinea fee in addition to the fee marked on the brief.'[23]

Then there was Marshall Hall, one of the most colourful, flamboyant – and no doubt expensive – barristers active at the turn of the century.[24] Although he did not practise regularly in the criminal courts, 'the legend of Marshall Hall,' it has been said, 'is the strongest ever woven round a figure at the Bar.'[25] However, his fortunes had fallen to a (relatively) low ebb during the first few years of the new century. He lost his parliamentary seat in the 1906 general election, and came out badly in a series of confrontations with members of the judiciary. His income fell, it was said, from £5,000 a year to little more than £1,000.[26] But his successful defence of a young artist, Robert Wood, in 1907 did much to revive his fortunes: 'Before long few sensational cases seemed complete without him.'[27]

Edward's case was difficult as well as sensational. 'Picture it for yourself!' recalled Smith Dorsett's clerk. 'A dead woman with *two* bullet wounds, one in her right arm; one in her head; the admissions to the doctor and the police – true, made by a drunken man. "Murder, you say, do you? That's all right." Reputation bad; character violent, previous convictions for savage assaults.'[28] Indeed, Marshall Hall thought at first that the best he could hope for was a verdict of manslaughter. He arrived in Stafford the day before the trial began, and it was then presumably that he and Edward met for the first time. They did not find it easy to work together. Marshall Hall was a fashionable, metropolitan barrister with a national reputation for flair and ingenuity, Edward a provincial businessman known best for his heavy drinking, uncertain temper and abusive relationships with women.[29] Smith Dorsett's clerk was dismissive: 'He was a thick-set, rather unprepossessing man, suffering badly from jaundice, as yellow as a guinea. He had lived out East [*sic*] for many years. He was a man of means, a brewer in Wolverhampton.'[30]

It was in the defence team's interests, obviously, to stress the difficulties of the case. But it would not be easy to defend Edward successfully. They decided, like Copeland, that it would be necessary to concede their client's respectability – and to blacken Ruth's name – in order to try to save Edward from the gallows. It was a strategy that Marshall Hall had used before. He had done so less than eighteen months previously, in the case that had revived his fortunes. He had defended Robert Wood, who was charged with murdering his lover, by listing his client's personal failings – and then denying that they had any relevance to the charges levelled against him.[31]

In Edward's case, the strategy meant conceding his client's personal and moral failings, presenting him as a weak man in thrall to an aggressive and dangerous woman. Indeed, Marshall Hall explained to the jury what he was doing, and why he had to do it:

He was sure everyone rebelled against the absolute necessity of having to attack the character of the poor dead woman. Pitiable and Zolaesque in character as were the details that had been revealed, he knew that he had the Judge's approval in doing what they did in order to show the true character of the deceased and her relations with Lawrence.[32]

Stafford Crown Court was crowded when the 'prisoner, on being arraigned, pleaded not guilty in a firm voice, and was allowed to be seated'.[33] F.W. Sherwood began setting out the case against Edward. He opened his address by declaring, conventionally enough, that he was sure that the (all-male) jury would approach their duties determined to reach a just verdict according to the evidence. He then got down to outlining the prosecution version of events, making clear (as Marshall Hall intended to) that Edward and Ruth had consistently flouted conventional notions of propriety. They had been 'intimate', he explained, for about five years, one result being that they had a three and a half year-old daughter (though she lived mostly with one of Ruth's sisters).

The prosecution would need to explore, Sherwood went on, 'more recent periods of their intimacy'. He took the jury back first to the previous September when, he said, 'there was bad blood between them'. Edward moved to George Street, Ruth moved out, Emma Stacey moved in – and there was an occasion, he alleged, when Edward fired at least one shot at Ruth. He then took the jury back to 22 December, the day that Emma Stacey and the servants left George Street as the result of 'some quarrel or misunderstanding'. Finally he took the court back to the day of the tragedy. Ruth was shot, Sherwood explained, some time between 8.50 and 9.50 in the evening. Shortly afterwards, Edward's next-door neighbours, the Boultons, heard him go out to fetch Dr Galbraith who, in turn called Dr Carter to accompany him to the scene of the incident. There they found Ruth, 'lying in the same room that Mattox [Kate Maddox] about an hour before had left her and prisoner.'

Turning towards Edward, Sherwood continued setting out the case against him. He explained that the defendant had been in an excited state, that he had been under the influence of drink, and that he had made a series of contradictory statements, some of which (such as 'I am glad I have done it') appeared highly incriminating. Sherwood explained too that inspectors Hill and Haynes had arrived at George Street, and taken Edward to the police station where they charged him with attempted murder, and later with murder. He explained finally that while he was at the police station, Edward asked to make a statement, made it, but then changed his mind and refused to sign it.

There were one or two other matters, Sherwood continued, which he 'must look upon'. There could be no doubt that the revolver which shot Ruth belonged to Edward Lawrence – and it was not a toy revolver either. Nor could there be any doubt that two separate shots had been fired. Another important matter, he continued, was the state of the room in which Ruth was found, because it bore on a possible defence that might be raised by Mr Marshall Hall. If self-defence were suggested, the jury would naturally expect to know whether there was any indication of a violent struggle between Edward and Ruth beyond that occasioned by the shooting. 'It was quite clear, and the true inference he submitted was, that no blows of any importance or severity had been dealt to Lawrence on this occasion.'

Prosecuting counsel went on to discuss what he termed 'one or two remarkable incidents with regard to the pistol'. Two shots had been fired, but when the police examined the gun, four of its five chambers had cartridges in them. It was possible, Sherwood suggested, that Edward had refilled one of the empty chambers either immediately after the shooting or during the time that Dr Galbraith went out to fetch Dr Carter.

'Was there any interval between the two doctors going out and when the police came?' wondered Judge Jelf.

'Yes, there was, my Lord.' The doctors, he explained, went out to collect dressings and to telephone for the police. But when the chamber was refilled, insisted Sherwood, was of less importance than the fact that it had been done, and that it must have been done by the prisoner.

In concluding, Sherwood reiterated that this was a case of murder. There was nothing to suggest suicide, nothing to suggest a serious struggle, and nothing to suggest that Ruth (a woman) had put Edward (a man) in such fear that he felt it necessary to do what he did.[34]

'I never saw a bottle'[35]

The prosecution then began presenting the evidence to support its case. The first witness it called was Ruth's sister, Theresa Harriman. She confirmed that Edward and Ruth had been living together intermittently for five years, and that they had a daughter who was now nearly four years old. Throughout her evidence she was at pains, naturally enough, to present her sister in the best light she could. She told the court about the incident the previous October when a policeman arrived at Edward's house as he and Ruth were quarrelling.

'Do you know how the policeman happened to come to the door that day?'

'No.'

'I suggest you knew Lawrence had sent for the policeman to turn your sister out.'

'I did not know it.'

'This bag that your sister struck Lawrence in the face with, was it what they call a string bag, that people go marketing with?'

'No, it was a hand-bag.'

'I want you to be careful about this answer. Was there a bottle of sherry in that bag, and did it cut Lawrence's face open?'

'No, sir; I never saw a bottle.'

'Did you see his eye cut by the blow that was given in your presence?'

'No, sir.'

'Did you know Lawrence had to go and have his eye dressed because of the injury your sister caused him?'

'No.'

On the contrary, she went on, she had told the police that Lawrence had twice tried to shoot her sister.

'Was your sister a woman of very violent temper?'

'She had a temper,' Theresa was forced to admit.

'Do you know that she had two or three times tried to stab this man?'

'No, sir.'

'Do you remember the incident about the hospital, when she was taken there with her hand and arm all cut to pieces?'

She admitted knowing Ruth had been taken to hospital, but denied any knowledge of how her injuries had been caused.

'Did you know she had put her arm through the window of the Board Inn, or had thrown a tankard?'

'No.'

'Did you ever hear of the blow she struck Mr Lawrence on the head with her umbrella, and broke the iron top, and left it in his head?'

'I never heard of it.'

'Do you mean to say you never heard of it?'

'No, sir, I have not.'

Theresa finished her evidence by denying knowing anything either about Ruth being discharged from the Coach and Horses in Selly Oak for trying to throw another barmaid through a window.[36]

Theresa was followed into the witness box by her sister, Kate Lewis, who also did what she could to protect Ruth's reputation. She told the court that on Christmas Eve 1908 she had gone with Ruth to help her clean Edward's house in George Street. Ruth, she stressed, was sober, but Edward was drunk.

It was a contrast that Marshall Hall did his best to undermine in cross-examination. But Kate gave as good as she got. Indeed, like other working-class witnesses, she seemed less intimidated by the legal process and the legal surroundings than one might expect. She denied noticing that her sister drank a good deal, and when asked whether she would call her sister 'a very sober woman', she had a ready response:

'She was always sober until she met Mr Lawrence, who taught her how to drink.'

Marshall Hall could not let this pass. He told Kate to face the jury:

'You have a strong feeling against Mr Lawrence in this matter?'

'All I am speaking is the truth.'

'Have you spoken the truth when you say Lawrence taught this woman to drink?'

'Yes, as true as God is above.'

Pressed further, Kate denied being aware that before Ruth met Edward, her sister 'was sleeping on a plank in a common lodging house, and was living an immoral life'.[37]

Marshall Hall's cross-examination of Ruth's sisters, concludes his biographer, was 'not perhaps so effective as Marshall's usual achievements in this line,' but it 'was the first suggestion of any defence at all.'[38]

'I will quieten you for good' [39]

The prosecution's next witnesses were two of the servants who had worked for Edward in the days leading up to Christmas. Edith Wardle told the court that she had started at George Street on 14 December, but that six days later she had walked out, along with Miss Stacey and the other two servants employed in the house. She returned the following day, she said, and took the opportunity to remove a loaded revolver from underneath Lawrence's bed.[40]

The other servant to give evidence was Kate Maddox, the last person other than Edward to see Ruth alive. The fifteen-year-old told the court that she knew Edward had a revolver, and had heard him threaten Miss Stacey on the day that she and the other servants walked out on him: 'If you don't keep quiet, I will quieten you for good.' This was not evidence, protested Marshall Hall. But Judge Jelf declined to exclude it because, he explained, it was Marshall Hall himself who had introduced the conduct of 'the woman Hadley'. Kate completed her testimony by telling the court what had happened on the evening of the shooting. Edward, she said, came in and tried to kiss her, and then began squabbling with Ruth (who had been drinking but could walk steadily) about who had been drinking the whisky from the jar. 'Not me, Ted,' Ruth had insisted.[41]

The next witness was Dr Galbraith. He repeated what he had said at earlier hearings. Edward had called to fetch him; they went back to Edward's house; he went out and found Dr Carter; and together they returned to discover Ruth lying on the floor seriously injured.

'Did prisoner say anything?' asked Sherwood.

'He said, "For God's sake do what you can for her. Be quick! Be quick!"'

'Anything else?'

'He said, "She is not dead, is she?" and later on "I did it in self-defence." He was excited and passionate, and he said, "I am glad I have done it. She is best dead." He added later, according to Galbraith, "You don't know what a wicked woman she is and what a life she has led me the last two months."'

Dr Galbraith went on to describe the state of the room in which they found Ruth.

'Did you notice any change in the condition of the room between your two visits?' asked the Judge.

'No, sir.'

The doctor recalled phoning the police and calling for an ambulance. It was his opinion, he said, that Edward had had something to drink, but that was not to say that he was drunk.

It was time for the defence team to put into practice its strategy of undermining Edward's character and reputation.

'Have you any doubt,' demanded Marshall Hall, 'that this man was a heavy and an habitual drunkard?'

'No.'

'Did he bear the evidence on his face of a man who drank hard?'

'Yes.'

'Have you heard that his brother drank himself to death?'

'I have.'

'And that his father and mother drank?'

'I have not heard.'

Marshall Hall then cross-examined the doctor about the effect that revolver shots might have when fired at the human body from various distances. Galbraith replied that in his opinion it was possible for a woman who was under the influence of drink to receive a wound like that on Ruth's arm and not to realise for some time that she had been injured.

Dr Galbraith was re-examined by the prosecution and then, at a quarter to six, the court adjourned until the following morning.

'All my ingenuity is wasted' [42]

In fact, Edward had to wait much longer than expected for the trial to recommence. It was no consolation, but legal precedent was about to be set. As soon as the court reconvened the next day, Judge Jelf reported that there was a problem: one of the jurors had been taken ill. The judge explained what he proposed to do. He would discharge the existing jury, recall the remaining eleven jurors, add a new juror, and thus create a new jury. He would then read the reconstituted jury his notes on the evidence already given, swear in the witnesses again, and ask them to alter or add to their evidence if they thought it necessary to do so.

When it was suggested to him that this would amount to asking leading questions, Jelf replied that leading questions were permissible if neither counsel nor the court raised any objection. After a certain amount of legal argument, it was agreed to put the judge's plan into action. The jury was duly discharged. The eleven remaining jurors stayed in the box, and a twelfth was called. The new jury was then sworn in, with the defence given the opportunity to challenge them. The witnesses were recalled, and Judge Jelf read out their evidence to them from his notes. He then asked them if what he had read out was correct, and gave both jury and counsel the opportunity to ask them questions. It was a process that took up the whole of Thursday morning.[43]

Eventually, the case resumed its normal course. Inspector Haynes and Elizabeth Wardle were recalled, the latter's testimony provoking a curious, juror-driven discussion of the ballistic evidence. Questioned by Marshall Hall, Elizabeth Wardle said that the revolver she took from under Edward's bed had been loaded with ball cartridges. Questioned by the judge, she looked at the gun's magazine, peered down the barrel, and confirmed that it was no longer loaded.

The gun was then passed, not to an expert witness, but to one of the jurors, who was a gunsmith.

The 'safety of the revolver is broken off,' observed the juror.

'So it is out of order.'

'Yes, my lord.'

This was an important point, observed Marshall Hall. The judge and the gunsmith-juror then examined the cartridge cases. The same drill, the juror observed, seemed to have been used on all the chambers, so that the same defect would probably be found on all of them.

'Then all my ingenuity is wasted,' conceded Marshall Hall, 'but it might have been an important point for me.'

'It is a very proper thing to inquire into,' the judge reassured him.[44]

The final witness for the prosecution was Dr Powell, the house surgeon at the general hospital. He informed the court of the results of the post-mortem examination he conducted on Ruth the morning following her death. Marshall Hall did his best to get him to agree that the revolver might have gone off accidentally while Edward and Ruth were struggling. (It was a line of questioning which suggested, of course, that the defence was attempting to secure an acquittal, rather than a verdict of manslaughter.[45])

'You are sure the deceased was not shot from behind?'

'Yes.'

'Supposing a woman holds a revolver, and another person tries to take it from her; and in the course of the struggle the revolver goes off, would this not account for the direction of the wound being such as we have heard in this case?'

'It depends altogether upon the way in which she was holding the revolver.'

Marshall Hall held up an empty revolver. He put his right hand on the trigger, and with his left hand turned the barrel towards his head.[46]

Dr Powell repeated that it would depend on the way in which the woman held the weapon. He did not think it would cause such a wound if the woman held the revolver with her finger on the trigger.

'Not if it was the case of a person holding the revolver and another person trying to struggle with her to take it off her?'

'In that case I think there would be blackening of the flesh.'

'Do you know the revolver can be discharged without pulling the trigger?'

'No.'[47]

The prosecution case was over. The situation did not seem at all good for Edward. According to Smith Dorsett's clerk, 'the general feeling in Stafford was that things looked very black against us.'[48] According to Marshall Hall's biographer, 'The jury seemed decidedly hostile, and the judge did not appear at all impressed by any of the points' that had been made.[49]

'Evidence of a somewhat sensational character'[50]

The trouble with the hagiographic tradition that has grown up surrounding Marshall Hall's courtroom performances is that it tends to exaggerate both the power of the prosecution arguments he faced, and the skill and effectiveness with which he combated them. 'No one could be as magnificent as Marshall Hall looks,' it was said of him. 'A handsome giant of a man who for a quarter of a century dominated the courts of England, he was undoubtedly the most famous defender in the annals of our legal history.'[51]

It is no surprise therefore to discover that Marshall Hall's persuasive powers in defending Edward Lawrence have been afforded almost superhuman status. In fact, according to one commentator, he only had to open his mouth: 'with his first sentence to the jury, in opening the defence, the atmosphere began to change.'[52] According to another, 'all was told in Marshall Hall's own inimitable style, with the packed court room and the spellbound jury hanging on his every word.'[53]

Hyperbole aside, Marshall Hall did manage, it seems, to bring about a distinct change in the atmosphere of the court. He began by making a short speech setting out the case for the defence. He would call witnesses, he promised, to show that Ruth was a violent woman, that she had often threatened Edward, and that she became more aggressive still after he had replaced her with another woman. Ruth's death, he reiterated, was a fatal accident, the result not of murder but of a drunken brawl.[54]

The first witnesses he called for the defence were the cabmen who had collected Ruth and her sister from Edward's house the previous October (when the policeman had been called). George Parker told the court that when he arrived, Ruth was 'helpless' and her sister was crying. He then provoked laughter by saying that when they reached the sister's house, he had to pull Ruth out of the cab by her legs. The judge was not amused. 'I am ashamed that anybody should laugh in a case like this. If there is anything of the kind again I will certainly have the Court cleared.'[55]

The next witness into the box was Isabella Pickett, Edward's housekeeper, who gave what the *Midland Counties Express* described as 'evidence of a somewhat sensational character'.[56] She said that she had known Ruth Hadley since November 1904, that on 5 May the following year Ruth had given birth to a child at her house, and that she subsequently went to work for Edward as his 'caretaker'.

'When you went there was Ruth Hadley living with Mr Lawrence?'

'No.'

'Did she come while you were there?'

'Yes.'

'Did you let her in once when Mr Lawrence was out?'

'Yes. She said Mr Lawrence had ordered her to come.'

'When he found her there what did he say?'

'He asked me why I had let her in, and said I had no right to have done so, and that I must not do it again.'

'What did you do?'

'I laid the table for them both, and after I left them in the dining room I heard a noise.'

'What did he say to you?' demanded Marshall Hall.

'He told me to me to take the woman away.'

'What did she do?'

'She went upstairs into Mr Lawrence's room and smashed an ornament from off the shelf. She next went into Mrs Lawrence's nursery and deliberately destroyed two of Mrs Lawrence's hats, which were in a box. This was in September, 1905.'

'That quarrel was forgiven?'

'Yes.'

'And things went pretty smoothly?'

'Yes; she had fetched her things from Ash-street?'

'Did she sleep there?' Judge Jelf interjected.

'Sometimes.'

'And after she moved her things she slept there every night?'

'Yes.'

'What were Hadley's habits so far as drinking was concerned?' demanded Marshall Hall.

Isabella responded exactly as he hoped.

'She drank very heavily; in fact, I never saw a young woman drink worse. She would drink from whatever bottle she came to first. Sometimes she would drink a small bottle of champagne before breakfast often before she came downstairs. She would drink beer, or spirits, or anything.'

'Was she a quiet, gentle woman?

'She was a very passionate and violent woman when in drink.'

'What sort of things did she say to Mr Lawrence?'

'Very vulgar and wicked.'

Marshall Hall changed tack slightly. 'Have you ever seen her do things?'

She knew what he was getting at. 'I saw her once level a revolver at Mr Lawrence.'

'Was it a loaded revolver?' wondered the judge.

'Yes.'

'Where was it usually kept?' resumed Marshall Hall.

'Under Mr Lawrence's bed.'

'What did he say to you about it when you first went there?'

'He said be careful with my young lady under the bed (meaning the revolver), and it will not hurt you.'

'Did Lawrence ever carry the revolver about with him?'

'Not to my knowledge.'

'What else has she done to him?'

'I saw her strike him once with her hand, and once with a silver cup. He did not strike her back.'

Marshall Hall was determined, not unnaturally, to get Isabella to round off her evidence with the most sensational example possible of Ruth's aggression and drunken violence.

'Do you remember Lawrence sending for his portmanteau as he wanted to go to Doncaster Races?'

'Yes, he sent a note by a cabman, but Hadley said he should not have it, and took the note from me. She also said, "I hope the train will run off the line and smash him."'

She was drunk, Isabella continued, when Edward returned home the following day, and they quarrelled about sleeping together, about her drinking too much, and about him supposedly sleeping with other women.

'After you had gone to bed did you hear anything?'

'I heard Lawrence call out. He said, "See what she has in her hand!"'

'Where was Ruth Hadley?'

'I got up, and saw her standing outside the bedroom in which they sometimes slept.'

'What was she doing?'

Isabella did not answer directly.

'While Mr Lawrence occupied her attention I rushed at her, pinned her by the throat, held her hand in which she had the revolver, and pushed her back into her own room and across the bed.'

'What became of the revolver?'

'Mr Lawrence took it away.'

'When she held the revolver did she say anything?'

'She said she would blow his brains out.'

Isabella was still being examined when the court rose for the day.[57]

Edward was probably feeling a little more hopeful. Of course, whatever the claims of Marshall Hall enthusiasts, we have no real way of assessing the impact that the two days' proceedings had upon the jury. However, it does not seem unreasonable to suggest that in so far as the afternoon's revelations had an impact on the jury, it would be to reinforce their – and the reading public's – impression of Ruth's heavy drinking and aggressive behaviour (which would be difficult, the defence hoped they would agree, for any man to cope with).

'Polluting the very source of justice'[58]

When Edward entered the dock the following morning, he certainly 'presented a more cheerful appearance than on the two previous days'. Although there was only a 'fair attendance of the general public', Margaret was again in the gallery. And as on the previous day, there was a delay in the proceedings, provoked this time by Marshall Hall observing that witnesses for the prosecution were entitled to protection from interference. Judge Jelf could not let the comment pass.

'Has anybody been doing anything of that kind?' he demanded.

'Unfortunately, yes,' Marshall Hall replied, 'I don't want to make too much of it, but ...'

'Anything like interference with any of the witnesses on either side who come here to tell us the truth in order that we may get to the bottom of this terrible story will be subject to the gravest possible punishment.'

'My remarks have nothing to do with the police or the solicitors on the other side, my lord.'

'I am quite sure,' remarked the judge, that 'the police in this county, or in any other county would not do anything of the kind.'

Marshall Hall was equally conciliatory. 'I ought to say, my lord, that the police engaged in this case have given us every possible assistance, and have shown us every courtesy.'

'I am sure they have. Unfortunately, sometimes outsiders take sides in these cases, and think they are justified in talking and tampering with witnesses. It is polluting the very source of justice. I am sorry that there are people who do these things, but if any of them come within my ken they will be subject to serious punishment.' [59]

'Perfectly easy and friendly terms' [60]

These exchanges, unlike those of the previous morning, did not occupy the court for very long. Isabella Pickett was recalled, and Marshall Hall continued his efforts to emphasise the volatility of Edward and Ruth's relationship with one another. He got Isabella to cast her mind back first to events towards the end of 1906. She recalled both that Ruth had been afraid to tell Edward that she had broken an expensive gun, and that they went away together for a holiday in Wales.

Isabella went on to give a more detailed account of what happened when she went to George Street on 27 December 1908 (just two days before Ruth died). Edward was having breakfast, she said. He had got up late, he explained, because he was not feeling well. Ruth, he claimed, had assaulted him on a number of occasions: she had attacked him with a 'chamber utensil', hit him in the face with a bottle of wine, and struck him on the back of the head with an umbrella. They were still quarrelling, recalled Isabella, over whether Edward was intending to invite Emma Stacey back into the house. If he did, threatened Ruth, she would make the 'crocks' and 'saucepans' fly; all he wanted, Edward retorted, was a quiet life. Edward went out, concluded Isabella, and Ruth began drinking whisky out of a stone jar. [61]

It was the prosecution's turn to cross-examine Isabella, and Sherwood did all he could to present Ruth – and her relationship with Edward – in a more favourable light. He got Isabella to agree that Ruth was 'well behaved' when she was not under the influence of drink. She appeared at times, Isabella conceded, to be fond of Lawrence, and he, in turn, 'always showed great respect for her'. When they were not arguing, they were on 'perfectly easy and friendly terms'. Indeed, according to Isabella's account, their relationship had acquired an uneasy equilibrium. Edward was 'terrified' of Ruth when she had been drinking, and Ruth was scared all the time that Edward would 'turn her and the child out' of the house.[62]

The defence then called a series of witnesses – a score or so in all – selected to present the court with a picture of a troubled and violent relationship, with Ruth much more aggressive than Edward. The neighbours, acquaintances, employees and former employees who followed Isabella into the witness box recounted incident after incident in which Ruth had attacked, or threatened to attack, her lover. Significantly, according to the standard account of the trial, 'not one of these witnesses could tell of any actual retaliation by the prisoner.'[63]

Cecil Frost's evidence was typical. A commission agent who had been lodging almost opposite one of the houses that Edward rented, he recalled an occasion the previous October when he had seen Edward and Ruth quarrelling in the street.

'She was excited and her manner threatening.'

'What effect had that on Lawrence?'

'He appeared to be afraid of her, and went into the house.'

'What did she do?'

'She went to the door and began kicking it, continuing for a few minutes. Lawrence let her in: but she came out again, and was still excited.' There had been many similar disturbances, added Frost. In his opinion, the deceased was a violent woman.[64]

The two final witnesses called by the defence were the doctors, Dr Bankier and Dr Mander. They reported, as we have seen before, that they had both examined Edward while he was on remand in Stafford Prison. They agreed that he had been drinking heavily at the time of Ruth's death, although he was now, believed Mander, of sound mind and in a fit condition to plead.[65]

'*I knew then there was going to be trouble*' [66]

Finally, on the fourth day of the trial, at about two o'clock in the afternoon, Marshall Hall put Edward into the witness box. It was a high-risk strategy. How would Edward perform? What would the jury make of him? Would they believe what he said? On the one hand, Edward was well educated, well spoken and self-assured. On the other hand, he could be obstinate and quick to anger: Marshall Hall himself found him difficult to deal with – on one occasion threatening to return to London if his client did not behave more appropriately. And Edward was by no means at his best. He was under immense pressure, he had been forced to stop drinking, he was suffering from jaundice, and he was said to be looking 'ghastly'.[67]

Nevertheless, Edward apparently gave his evidence in a cool, controlled and convincing fashion.[68] This is the *Birmingham Gazette and Express*'s account of what he said.

> Prisoner gave evidence on oath. He was taken through the history of his life, and detailed how he became acquainted with Hadley, saying that he was introduced to her, and that he took her to Birmingham. He had lived with her off and on, and he corroborated the various incidents which had been spoken of by the witnesses for the defence. He met the girl in Queen's-square, Wolverhampton, on Christmas Eve. She asked him if he had got anyone in the house. He said that he had not, and she begged to be allowed to go back to live in the house. In a weak moment he consented and gave her the latchkey.[69]

Finally Edward came to the day of the tragedy. Ruth, he said, had spent the previous night at George Street, and then cooked him lunch.

'What happened next?' demanded Marshall Hall.

'I was in town the whole of the afternoon visiting my different houses. I got home about eight o'clock.'

He came in, he said, sat down, had a drink – and began quarrelling with Ruth over whether or not she was drunk.

'I sat down at the other end of the room. She became calmer and told Mattox [Kate Maddox] to go home. Shortly afterwards Mattox left. I don't know the reason for her getting rid of Mattox, but the moment the girl left the throwing of things began in earnest.'

'I tried to persuade her to be quiet; but she got worse and worse. I then thought of the revolver. I went upstairs to see if it was there. As I was going upstairs she said, "You need not go up there. I know what you are after. I've got it." I knew then there was going to be trouble.'

'I came down. She pointed it at me, and after a tussle I got it from her. I put it in my pocket, and I told her to go. Her only answer was a further volley of crocks. I told her if she did not desist I should shoot her. She struck me again with the tongs ... I took the revolver from my pocket, and fired well wide of her to frighten her.'

'Did you know that the bullet had struck her?' demanded Marshall Hall.

'No.'

'What did she do?'

'She became quieter.'

He went upstairs, he claimed, to replace the revolver.

'As she did not appear to be going I went from the front room to the middle room. The moment I got outside the door she pointed the revolver at me. She had evidently got it from upstairs.'

'Was the bed in order when you went up?'

'Yes.'

'And it would have had to be put in this order to find the revolver?'

'Yes.'

'What happened,' demanded Marshall Hall again.

'She pointed the revolver at me. She was pressing the trigger, and I could see the hammer rising. I knew my only chance then was to go for her. I dashed in and got the revolver with my left hand by the barrel, and turned it from me just as it went off.'

'What happened then?'

'She fell.'

Marshall Hall continued to lead Edward in the direction that he wanted.

'Was your hand on it as well as hers?'

'I had hold of the barrel only, but not the stock.'

'What did you think she fell from?'

'I thought she was drunk. I had no idea she was shot. I then picked up the revolver and put it in my pocket. I said, "Get up; let's have no foolery."'

'Then you saw the hole in the temple?'

'Yes, and as soon as I did I ran for the doctor. I went to the front door, but there was no key, and it was locked.'

'You were very much upset and distressed?'

'I must have been.'

'Had you any intention of hurting the woman when you fired the first shot?'

'No.'

'And you have no explanation as to the second shot, except what you have given?'

'No.'

'Did you ever shoot at this woman with the intent to kill her?'

'Never in my life.'

At this point, the judge declared that the court would adjourn for a short time, before reconvening for cross-examination and re-examination.[70]

'Things that were not to be taken seriously'[71]

Half an hour later, Edward re-entered the witness box, to face what he – like any defendant – would expect to prove a considerable ordeal, cross-examination by the prosecution.

He confirmed, *inter alia*, that it was his custom to keep a revolver under his pillow. But he had 'never used it outside', he insisted, 'except now and again in the backyard'. He had only purchased one set of cartridges, and that had been twenty years before.

'And you have many left now?' asked the judge.

'Yes.'

He denied ever using the revolver in self-defence, and denied too ever having used it to threaten Emma Stacey.

Sherwood moved on to his relationship with Ruth.

'Were you in fear of Hadley when she threatened you?'

'I was the later part of the time.'

Sherwood did his best to counter the impression that it was Ruth who was the aggressor.

'She looked after you all right when she was well?'

'Yes,' agreed Edward.

'And when she was drunk she said things that were not to be taken seriously?'

'When the worse for drink she was not particular what she said.'

'Why, if you stood in fear of her, did you not break with her for good?'

'I tried to do so on many occasions.'

'Then do you suggest that she forced herself on you?'

'I do.'

'But she was away when Stacey lived with you?'

'Yes.'

He turned his attention to Edward's behaviour.

'You were unfortunately often drunk?'

'Yes.'

'When she threatened you and used violent language, had you been in the habit of replying in the same strain?'

'I may have done so occasionally,' conceded Edward.

Finally Sherwood moved to the events of 29 December. But despite his best efforts, he could not get Edward to alter his account of what happened between the time he came home to George Street and the time Kate Maddox left him alone with Ruth.

The case was adjourned for the day.[72]

It had gone as well as Edward and his legal team could reasonably have hoped. Edward had given his evidence clearly, he had stood up well to cross-examination, and he seemed to have made a good impression on the judge and the jury. Indeed, it has been suggested that from this point onwards, the judge 'addressed the prisoner as "Mr" Lawrence, rather than as "Lawrence," as he had done before.'[73]

'A very torrent of eloquence'[74]

There were no delays the following morning, and Marshall Hall began by telling the jury that they could reach one of three possible verdicts: murder, manslaughter or not guilty. He would be pressing them, he made it perfectly clear, to return a verdict of 'not guilty'. He stressed that they were not trying Edward for drink, for immorality, or for being a fool and leaving his wife and family for other women. In fact, he noted, Edward's wife had stood by him, and he hoped that if his client were acquitted he would devote the rest of his life to making his wife and children happy and doing the best he could to make amends for the misery he had caused them.

He turned to Ruth's character and behaviour, describing her as 'a reckless, violent, impossible woman, dangerous to the last degree, of a nature which brooded in secret over fancied wrongs, and finally blossomed out into violence which makes resistance impossible.' It was, of course, stupid of Edward to take back such a woman, but men did these things, and would go on doing them 'to the end of the chapter'.

Marshall Hall drew the jury's attention next to what he described as Ruth's awful, ominous words, 'He will either kill me or I'll kill him.' Indeed, he claimed that she had threatened to give Edward an 'advertisement' he would never forget to the longest day he lived. 'She has done it!' concluded Marshall Hall theatrically.

For the rest of his life, whatever your verdict may be, he will have to stand before the world bearing the stigma of being the man who stood his trial for wilful murder at Stafford Assizes in March, 1909. She has given him an advertisement which he will never forget – she has!

Finally he moved to the events of 29 December, suggesting that Ruth's shooting was the almost inevitable culmination of Edward's and Ruth's drunken excesses and increasingly volatile relationship. What happened, he claimed, was that Edward snatched his revolver from Ruth and fired it in order to frighten her, but because he was 'not sober' he caught her on the arm. He hid the revolver, Ruth found it, and there was another struggle in which he accidentally shot his lover in the head. The climax to Marshall Hall's oration was his now celebrated comparison between trying a man for his life and weighing something on a pair of scales.

> The scales of justice were held by a master hand. His duty was
> to hold the scales level, and see that no atom of prejudice was
> introduced. In the one scale unseen by human eye, but there with all
> its weight, with all its value, was that which belonged to the prisoner;
> in the other scale was the weight of the prosecution. If the balance
> was struck so level that honestly in their minds the jury could not see
> which scale was nearer to the ground, it was their duty to remember
> that the invisible weight of that invisible substance – the presumption
> of the prisoner's innocence, the right of every man to be regarded as
> innocent until proved guilty – forced down that scale until the other
> soared into the air.

'I leave it in your hands,' he concluded. 'Try this man upon the evidence, and upon the evidence, with the help of God, I ask you to say that this man, Edward Lawrence, is not guilty.'[75]

When Marshall Hall sat down, he had had been speaking for just over two hours. It had been a bravura performance, and Edward must have been buoyed by what he had heard. The reporters covering the case were certainly impressed. It was 'an able and eloquent speech', declared the *Staffordshire Advertiser*.[76] The *Midland Counties Express* was particularly enthusiastic: 'Mr Hall proceeded to recount the events in the story, the spectators in court literally hanging on his words, which fell in a very torrent of eloquence.'[77]

'Not guilty'[78]

Sherwood could do little to dent the momentum that Marshall Hall had generated. He spoke for about an hour and a half, but judging from the amount of coverage his speech received in the press, his efforts were much less compelling than Marshall Hall's. Not only was he up against one of the most charismatic members of the bar, but he felt it necessary to abandon the charge of murder, and ask the jury to reach instead a verdict of manslaughter. He concluded, rather weakly, that before the jury could accept a plea of self-defence, they would have to be satisfied that there had been a real necessity for Lawrence to act as he had.[79]

The court adjourned for half an hour. All that was left now was for Judge Jelf to give his summing up. Jelf, like Sherwood, spoke for an hour and a half, and he made it perfectly clear that he thought Edward was innocent. He admitted that he had been extremely doubtful about the new principle of allowing prisoners to give evidence on their own behalf. But he had changed his mind: 'If this was the only case he ever tried he should be thankful for the change, because without the opportunity thus presented it was unlikely the prisoner, who was the only person present at the tragedy, could have escaped at least a verdict of manslaughter.'[80]

The jury retired to consider their verdict just before half past four, the foreman asking permission to take the revolver with them. Edward, who had been making notes during the afternoon, discussed the situation with his legal team, before going below 'pending the crucial moment'.

After just under half an hour, the jury returned, and delivered its verdict: 'Not guilty'.

It was then that the judge gave Edward the 'few words of advice' that were cited at the beginning of the book.

> Before I discharge you, I want to add a few words of advice to those which your brilliant counsel have already, I have no doubt, given to you. You have had a most terrible lesson. You have been mixed up with a terrible tragedy. You have had now, in the time you have been in prison, an opportunity of seeing what is the difference between a man with the use of his senses and his feelings which God had given him unprepared for that horrible fiend of drink; and you have also had the opportunity of seeing how your wife has been so grievously wronged some time ago, and who yet has been ready to forgive you. And I think it is possible that if you turn over a new leaf you may yet have a happy time with your wife and children, and that you may be forgiven by God for your past life. I say this for your family's sake, because I think, having acted this awful experience, you must feel how much all that has happened has been due to your own habits and immorality; and I hope that what I have said before will bear fruit in your after life.[81]

'Lawrence replied, in a clear voice, "Thank you, my lord," and having been handed his hat by a warder, immediately left the dock, and was met by Mrs Lawrence and one or two friends.'[82]

Edward was a free man. Although it was still snowing heavily when he, his wife Margaret and several friends left the shire hall at half past five, a large crowd of people had waited in the hope of seeing the man who had undergone such 'a terrible experience'. Edward and his party adjourned to the Café Royal opposite, where they had tea in one of the side rooms. Edward, not surprisingly, was 'instantly recognized by those at table'.[83]

Despite the snow, Edward and Margaret managed to get back to Wolverhampton that same evening. He went to the Board Inn, the public house to which he so often gravitated. Once again, he was the centre of attention, a large crowd, some of them drunk, hanging around in the hope of catching a glimpse of the town's newest celebrity.[84] Some Wulfrunians, it seems, were convinced of Edward's innocence.[85] But some were not. When Edward's landlord read of his acquittal, he remarked that he 'was much astonished at the verdict [...] I should think he thinks himself a very lucky man.'[86]

11

'The nobs all dropped him'[1]

Edward's reputation had surely sunk as low as it possibly could. Wolverhampton's newspaper-reading public had known for some years that he was a heavy drinker, that he had been unfaithful to his wife, and that she had divorced him. But press coverage of the trial meant that even those who lived further afield and/or believed him innocent of murder, now knew more than they could ever have imagined about his drinking, his domestic arrangements and his sexual exploits. He had breached, it is clear, all the major tenets of Victorian middle-class masculinity, with its emphasis upon 'a punishing work ethic, a compensating validation of the home, and a restraint of physical aggression'.[2]

Many, of course, did not think Edward innocent of Ruth's murder. It was not just his landlord who felt him lucky to be acquitted.[3] So too, predictably enough, did many members of Ruth Hadley's family.[4] So too, more tellingly, did Kate Maddox, the young servant who was the last person – other than Edward – to see Ruth alive.[5] Moreover, it seems likely that many of those who heard – or heard about – Judge Jelf's summing up at the trial would conclude that Edward was acquitted, not because he was innocent, but because he was well enough off to be able to engage an outstanding advocate to argue his case.[6] Whatever the reasons, recalled Kate Maddox, as soon as the verdict was announced, those she regarded as 'the nobs' all 'dropped him'.[7]

Not that Edward made much attempt to rebuild his damaged reputation. He resumed his drinking – in public as well as in private – as soon as he was able to do so.[8] Indeed, within a few days of his acquittal, he was charged, it is said, with assaulting a man in a Wolverhampton pub.[9] Within a few weeks more, he was charged, there is firm evidence, with three offences of refusing to pay his cab fares – in one case leaving the driver out of pocket to the – enormous – sum of 25 shillings.[10]

'Public examination in bankruptcy' [11]

This was both stupidity and profligacy. But it was the trial, of course, that posed the real threat to Edward's finances. It cannot have been easy for him to run his business while he was in custody, and by the time he was released some suppliers and customers might well have become wary of dealing with a self-confessed drinker and philanderer. But whatever the pressures upon him, he remained as belligerent as ever. After stalling for six months over the rent due on George Street, he finally paid the £12 that he owed towards the end of 1909. But he could not resist taunting the agent handling the matter: 'As you are so assiduous in your client's interests! it almost makes one regret that one has not property to place in your hands. The only regret I have in the matter is that the law does not allow you to issue writ before the money is due.' [12]

However satisfying Edward found it, such sarcasm could not help stem his financial problems or prevent them from becoming more widely known. Indeed, at the same time as he was prevaricating privately over the payment of his rent, he was disposing of some of his assets,[13] and taking a decision that amounted to a semi-public admission of his personal and financial difficulties. Although his three sons had been at Wolverhampton Grammar School for barely a year, he decided that it would be best to move them elsewhere. The shame of the trial, the costs it generated, and the burden of paying the boys' fees (of just under £40 a year) convinced him that he should not, or could not, re-enrol them for the school year 1909–10.[14]

There was further indignity besides. Edward's financial failings were paraded for all to see when the Wolverhampton Gas Company issued a bankruptcy notice against him in October 1910.[15] It was a blow not just to his reputation for financial competence but also to any more broadly based standing that he still enjoyed in the local community. For while it might be true that English bankruptcy law provided 'an efficient mix of tolerance towards honest debtors and strictness towards fraudulent agents',[16] it invariably tended to humiliate and undermine those who fell within its clutches.[17]

The bankruptcy proceedings took several months, and were reported dutifully and sometimes very fully in the pages of the local press. The Gas Company's petition against Edward was published in the *Express and Star*, the *Midland Counties Express*, and the *London Gazette*.[18] Then at the beginning of December, the *Midland Evening News* reported that Edward had been called to his 'public examination in bankruptcy', only for the case to be 'set down for a future date'.[19]

The adjudication of the case in January 1910, it must be said, aroused little press interest. But three months later, the *Express and Star* carried a detailed report of the attempt made by three creditors to persuade the trustee of Edward's estate to reverse his decisions as to which debts were to be paid under the bankruptcy. The hearing, which was held at Wolverhampton County Court, revealed a good deal both about Edward's financial circumstances and about his state of mind. Newspaper reports of the proceedings provide an indication, for example, of the legal costs that Edward had incurred in defending himself against the charge of murder. He had to pay his solicitor Copeland as well as his three barristers Smith Dorsett, Benyon Harris and Marshall Hall. Copeland alone submitted a bill for well over £1,000, four times what Edward's basic salary had been when he had been employed in the family business.[20]

Newspaper reports also provide an indication of Edward's belligerent resilience. He had killed his lover, been tried and acquitted of murder, faced local ostracism and been declared bankrupt. But he remained, in public at least, as pugnacious and self-confident as ever. When Copeland's case had been dealt with, the court turned to a claim by a local 'commission agent', Mr Kidson, who maintained that Edward owed him £15 following his purchase of public houses from the Manchester Brewery Company in 1905. Edward immediately became embroiled in a fractious exchange with Kidson's counsel, Mr Foster, which culminated in the latter complaining that Edward was asking him silly questions.

'Then don't ask me silly questions,' retorted Edward, adding, with heavy sarcasm, that if he was told what to say he would say it.

At this point, Judge Smith intervened: 'You must treat Mr Foster with respect, otherwise I shall send you to Stafford for twenty-one days.'

Even a threat as pointed as this did not deter Edward, and a short while later Judge Smith again felt it necessary to warn him to keep his temper.

Edward had further minor altercations with counsel before, at the very end of the proceedings, asking the judge for permission to address the court. He explained that he wished to appeal against the decision, made in the final case of the day, to pay the bulk of the claim brought by an architect whom he had hired.

'I am in a very difficult position, and do not understand the legal form.'

The solicitor representing the trustee of the estate rose to speak.

'Wait a bit! Wait a bit!' protested Edward, determined to have the last word. 'I am here for advice.'[21]

'Nauseating details' [22]

The press also reported two highly embarrassing claims that Margaret and her father made against Edward's estate. Edward's and Margaret's reconciliation, such as it was, in the wake of his acquittal did not last very long. Indeed, their relationship deteriorated so badly that Margaret and her father apparently felt that there was no chance of a rapprochement, and concluded therefore that their best course was to pursue legal action.

There were complications. Because Edward was now a bankrupt, some of Margaret's claims needed to be made, not against him, but against the trustee in bankruptcy. In the first case, which was dealt with in April 1910, Margaret's father submitted a claim for £51, the maintenance payments he alleged Edward owed him for the five months during which his daughter and grandchildren stayed with him after Edward had assaulted Margaret in the summer of 1905. Margaret, once again, proved an appealing and effective witness, drawing, as in her earlier court appearance, upon prevailing notions of what constituted appropriate male and female behaviour.

'Why did you leave him?' Margaret was asked.

Although counsel for the trustee protested that it was not necessary to introduce 'nauseating details', Margaret managed to explain that 'she had been badly knocked about, and was afraid of further violence'. The trustee's barrister pressed on, reading an extract from a letter that Edward had written to Margaret: 'As you have made no application for money, I have taken it that you have not been in need of it.'

Judge Smith was indignant: 'I should always conclude that my wife was in need of money.' [23]

Edward was back in court, and back in the papers, two months later when Margaret appealed against the trustee's decision to reject a claim she had made for £3,597. It was another complicated case. Her claim was based on a deed that Edward had signed at the beginning of 1907 agreeing to pay her an annuity (in effect a divorce settlement) of £136 a year. Margaret argued that the deed was still valid; the trustee countered that it was invalid because she and Edward had been reconciled and had begun living together again. (She had taken him home with her immediately following his acquittal and, as we shall see, there was a later, abortive attempt at reconciliation at Kidderminster railway station.)

Even Judge Smith, who was hearing this case too, conceded that he had some sympathy for Edward, in as far as 'the fact that he had been tried for murder had been alluded to in those as in other proceedings relating to his bankruptcy.' However, the judge's sympathy was strictly limited. He did not trust Edward. 'He did not believe his testimony with regard to the actions of his wife, nor should he do so with regard to the actions of any other woman. Lawrence had admitted that he was drunken, and that his relations with other women were loose.'[24] Judge Smith's view was that there had been no reconciliation of any kind prior to Edward's acquittal in March 1909, and that when Margaret took him home with her on his acquittal it was only because he had nowhere else to go. And even then, he believed, reconciliation and cohabitation were 'procured by the duress of her husband, and although her body was consenting he found that her mind was not'. He decided, after making the necessary calculations, that Margaret should win her claim, but for £1,750 rather than £3,597.[25]

Margaret pressed on, seeming now, like Edward, to be almost beyond embarrassment. In her determination to get what she thought she was entitled to, she brought two – equally well publicised – claims against Edward himself. In the first, which was dealt with at West Bromwich Police Court in November 1910, she applied for a maintenance order on behalf of herself and her children. She explained that there had been a further – fraudulent – attempt at reconciliation, Edward inviting her to live with him in Kidderminster, the town fifteen miles south of Wolverhampton, to which he had moved a year or so previously.[26] But when Margaret arrived at Kidderminster station, there to meet her with Edward was Emma Stacey, his long-time lover and mother of one of his illegitimate children.

Even this was not the end of the matter. Edward again asked Margaret to live with him, but she refused because, as she pointed out (perfectly reasonably), she could not possibly trust him. Eventually an agreement was brokered, whereby Edward undertook to pay Margaret the sum of £2 a week. 'The Stipendiary,' reported the *Kidderminster News*, 'observed that he hoped the settlement would be final.' 'There had been enough spent in litigation to have kept Mrs Lawrence and her family for a considerable time.'[27]

It may be significant therefore that Edward chose not to appear – or even to be represented – when Margaret took him back to court less than two months later. Perhaps even he was beginning to balk at the cost and the public exposure of his financial and other failings. Not that his absence stemmed the flow of adverse publicity. In an escalation of their dispute over alimony payments, Margaret applied to the stipendiary magistrate for a warrant for Edward's arrest, claiming that he was already in arrears on the separation order she had obtained the previous November. She had not intended to apply for the warrant, she insisted, until Edward's bankruptcy had been settled. But he had paid her no money at all until he was warned about this application for his arrest – whereupon he sent her a cheque for just £2. After some discussion, the magistrate decided that the court should do as Margaret requested and issue a warrant for Edward's arrest. In one local newspaper's report on what it called this 'Local Domestic Muddle', it was remarked, with more than a little understatement, that Edward Lawrence's 'affairs have repeatedly been under public scrutiny'.[28]

Meanwhile, back in Wolverhampton, Edward came in for yet more press attention. He was charged with assaulting a Wolverhampton merchant, Benjamin Smith, a councillor who had been a member of the committee of inspection dealing with his bankruptcy. Summoned twice to appear before Wolverhampton Police Court, Edward claimed first that he was too ill to attend, and then that he was out of town.[29] Eventually, in the middle of March, he made it to court. He was found guilty and fined forty shillings plus costs, whereupon in a typically derisive and flamboyant gesture, designed presumably to show that he was still a man of means, 'the money, £2 14s. 6d., in all, was paid out of a £5 note.'[30]

At the same time as he was defending himself, unsuccessfully, against the charge of assaulting councillor Smith, he was recalled for further examination by Wolverhampton Bankruptcy Court. Once again he pleaded illness, and once again the hearing was adjourned.[31] The delayed examination eventually took place towards the end of March, when Edward denied deliberately concealing assets from the court, and denied too knowing who councillor Smith was when he 'pushed' him. He was as belligerent as ever.

'Will you say what was the origin of the dispute?' asked the official receiver.

'Oh, that's better,' retorted Edward.

'Mr Registrar,' complained the receiver, 'I entirely object to the impertinent way in which the bankrupt speaks.'

Registrar: 'You have great latitude so far. Unless you submit yourself to the Court to be examined I shall have to report you to the Judge, and I think you will probably have gathered the kind of order he will make.'

Debtor: 'I have no other desire, but the manner in which the questions are put …'

Registrar: 'The questions are put in a perfectly proper manner, and you are there to answer them.'

Debtor: 'But the insinuations I submit are …'

Registrar: 'Answer the questions.'[32]

'A Gilbert and Sullivan opera'[33]

Whatever embarrassment Edward suffered in court, it never seemed to deter him for long from embarking upon yet more legal battles. And whatever plans he might have had for rehabilitating his reputation, they did not inhibit him from using the legal system in ways likely to lay him open to yet further criticism. In fact, he fought his corner so doggedly that there was scarcely a month during 1910 and early 1911 when his growing range of legal entanglements did not find him in court, and in the pages therefore of the Kidderminster papers.

He became embroiled first in a series of disputes over the repairs and alterations he was having carried out to the house he had bought. Within a year of year or so of moving to Kidderminster, one of his builders, Charles Walker, became so frustrated with Edward that he obtained a court judgement against him for the money which he said he was owed. Edward claimed in turn that he knew nothing about the hearing at which the judgement had been made. Therefore what was needed, he argued, was a new trial at which he would be able to defend himself against this unfounded claim.

Edward's application for a new trial was heard in August 1910. His reputation preceded him. He is 'an extraordinary man', complained Walker's counsel, 'constantly in litigation'. As if to prove the point, Edward and the judge became entangled almost immediately in a war of words over whether or not Edward had received the summons which the court had sent him.

The Judge (to Lawrence): 'If the letter was posted the law assumes that you got it.'

Lawrence: 'The only notification I had was from Mr Ivens [Walker's counsel].'

The Judge: 'You have said that several times. We must have things definitely proved. If the officials of the court prove that the letter was posted, the law assumes that you have had it.'

Lawrence: 'The law cannot assume I had it.'

The Judge: 'It does so.'

Lawrence: 'It is an assumption, so why should I suffer in consequence?'

The Judge: 'You appear to be most unfortunate.'

Lawrence: 'I am terribly so.'[34]

A few months later, another of the builders Edward had hired, Richard Davies, took him back to court.[35] Davies had started work for Edward before the bankruptcy proceedings against him had begun. When Davies heard the news, he was worried, not unnaturally, that he might not be paid for the work he had done, let alone for any jobs that he might take on in the future. Edward was reassuring: 'I've plenty of money, and I will pay you week by week.'[36] Davies stayed on, and for a while the architect overseeing the work, Thomas Lowrie,[37] authorised stage payments as Edward had promised. However, the payments ground to a halt, and Davies sued Edward for £68 of the £200 that it had been agreed he should be paid for undertaking repairs and alterations to the house.[38]

The case came to the county court early in 1911. Edward was back to his old self. He hired a solicitor, entered a counter-claim for £125, attended the hearing, and demanded the right to speak.

'Who are you?' demanded the judge.

'I am the defendant.'

'No, you cannot be heard. You have a solicitor.'[39]

The case was adjourned for a month. When the court reconvened, the two sides presented conflicting evidence about almost everything: from the details of the contract, to the quality of the workmanship, to the way in which payments had been made. Edward followed his builder and architect into the witness box, insisting not only that he had kept to his contract with Davies but also that he had paid him money on account. He had done so, he insisted, despite the fact that he often had cause for complaint about the quality of the work being done: the timber used for the doors and windows had not been properly matured, and some of his valuable pictures had been damaged. It was quite true, Edward agreed, that he had received £1,000 from his trustee in bankruptcy, and true too that he had spent it all. However, he reacted more aggressively – and more characteristically – towards the end of his cross-examination. The conduct of the case, he protested, was like a Gilbert and Sullivan opera.[40]

The case was adjourned yet again, this time until the end of March. When the court reconvened for a second time, it heard further evidence about the work which had been done to Edward's new house. Walker, who was a timber merchant as well as a builder, testified that he had supplied his fellow builder Davies with 'all reasonably seasoned timber'. There was further confusion when the two architects called as expert witnesses contradicted one another as to the quality of the work that had been completed. Eventually the judge reached his decision, awarding Davies most, but not all, of his claim, and dismissing Edward's counter-claim.[41]

The disputes between Edward and his tradesmen had still other ramifications. Edward's builder-cum-timber merchant, Charles Walker, now sued his architect, Thomas Lowrie, claiming that he was still owed £8 for the work he had done. Edward was involved, on this occasion, only as a witness but, as so often, he reacted belligerently to the pressures – and opportunities – of appearing in the witness box. He did not seem able to resist the lure of a platform on which to assert himself both against his personal enemies and against the legal establishment that had helped to lay him low.

Lowrie's counsel began questioning Edward about the wood that had been used to build a large 'fowl-pen' in the garden of his house. At this point, Lowrie made what was described as 'an audible observation'.

'I'll knock your head off outside,' responded Edward.

'You are not here to make remarks of that kind,' remonstrated the judge.

'You didn't hear, your Honour, the remark the man Lowry made to me.'

When Edward's barrister confirmed that Lowrie had said something, the architect was ordered to leave the court.

Edward now did his best to be ingratiating, explaining that, 'he did not wish anything which was not correct, but it was very galling to stand there and hear insulting remarks made to him.'

When Lowrie's barrister resumed his questioning, he did his best to unsettle Edward: was it not true, he demanded, that Edward carried out cock-fighting in his large fowl-pen?

Edward denied the charge – adding that the judge would need to explain to counsel that cock-fighting was illegal.

Even the court's conclusions seemed to exemplify the confusion into which Edward's legal incursions so often seemed to entrap those caught up in them. 'The judge held that there was no evidence of direct authority given by Lawrence to Lowry, gave judgement for the plaintiff against Lowry, and dismissed the action against Lawrence, with costs, and a certificate for Counsel.'[42]

'A matter of persecution'[43]

Edward became embroiled in several other disputes. The local police, the company supplying him with coal, and even one of the servants working for him seemed to take it in turns to take him to court. Whether or not their grievances were justified, the effect of the ensuing courtroom battles was, it appears, to aggravate Edward, to reinforce his sense of persecution and to compound his reputation for irresponsibility and disreputability.

The first case was trivial indeed. The Kidderminster police summoned Edward at the county petty sessions for not having a collar on his dog, and for failing to keep the animal under proper control. Petty, Edward felt not unreasonably, was *le mot just*. Replying to the first charge, he 'complained of the attention which of late he had received from the hands of the police and others. He felt that he had been getting rather more attention than was his share. Some people might regard that as an honour, but he felt it was a nuisance.'

Responding to the second charge, he asked the police constable who had found his dog, 'why he was sometimes prowling around his grounds at unearthly hours.' The exchange developed into a vintage, albeit brief, example of Edward's sarcastic persistence.

P.C. Broad: 'What do you mean?'

The Defendant said it was an English word he had used.

The Chairman said the question had nothing to do with the case.

But Edward would not let the matter rest.

'The Defendant submitted that there was no proof that the dog was dangerous. It was purely a matter of persecution. Why didn't the police do their duty in other directions and not persecute him. It spoke highly for the morals of the district that the police had nothing else to do than to bring such paltry cases before the Court.'[44]

However confrontational and articulate Edward was in his defence, it seemed to be open season upon him. At the very same sitting of the county court at which he had applied for a new trial in his dispute with Charles Walker, he was summoned by the Cannock Chase Coal Company for not paying for fuel it had delivered to him. Edward did not dispute that he owed the company payment for one load of coal and one of coke, but he denied knowing anything at all about a second delivery. It was a matter of agency, the judge explained, calling 'attention to the point that the goods were ordered by one person and the plaintiffs were suing another person.' It was the sort of nicety that Edward, like any lawyer (or barrack-room lawyer), would try to exploit. He accepted that the second load of coal had been ordered by his 'sort of housekeeper', Mrs Peplow, but 'denied that she 'had any authority from him to order any coal'. But still Edward lost the case, the coal company securing a verdict against him for £3 2s. 6d.[45]

Just two days later, Edward found himself back before the same court. This was a much more serious case. Edward had replaced his 'sort of housekeeper', Mrs Peplow, with a Birmingham woman, Fanny Thompson. She soon found him difficult to work for; matters came to a head, she claimed, when he told her – in a telling reversal of conventional priorities – to take his son to the workhouse, and to collect his gun from the pawnshop. By this time, Fanny was scared, she said, to work for him. But she proved far from a passive victim. She went to see the chief constable of the borough, and persuaded him to send a constable, PC Bevan, to accompany her when she returned to Edward's to collect her belongings and outstanding wages. When Bevan's presence failed to prevent Edward swearing at her and hitting her, she took out a summons against him for assault.

The press had a field day: 'Extraordinary Proceedings on Bewdley Hill', 'Extraordinary Allegations Against A Gentleman'.[46] So too did Fanny's counsel: 'the facts in this case disclosed conduct on the part of the defendant which seldom came before a Court. He should be able to show that that conduct had been most reprehensible indeed.' Edward was drinking heavily, he claimed, which put Fanny 'in bodily fear of him'. When she returned to collect her wages and belongings, Edward 'struck her with his clenched fist on the bosom, from the effects of which she had not yet recovered.'

When Edward, who was representing himself, began his cross-examination of Fanny, he clashed immediately, one after the other, with Fanny, with Fanny's counsel and with the chairman of the bench.

'If you are afraid of me,' he asked Fanny, 'what brought you in my bedroom that night?'

Fanny declined to answer.

'Which night do you mean?' demanded the clerk of the court.

'The night of entry to my house.'

'Counsel rose to object to the defendant's line of cross-examination, and was received with the observation from the defendant: I have given you every liberty and never said a word. I am going to talk now.'

Edward persisted, Fanny's counsel objected, but Edward pressed on with his line of questioning. 'The Chairman said the Bench required the defendant to conduct his case in a proper way.'

Undeterred, Edward continued to irritate and provoke until the hearing drew to a close. He was innocent of any assault, he concluded, his rhetoric rising to new heights.

> However, whatever happened, he was a Briton, and would accept anything that came to him in the way of allegation; but in this particular matter he gave the Bench his word of honour – and he swore it by all that was good and holy – that he had never been within sufficient distance of the complainant of the day in question which could justify any such charge. Though he might be good or bad, he had not lost all faith.[47]

It was vintage Edward, but all to no avail. It was announced that, 'the Bench had not the slightest hesitation in convicting the defendant. He had committed an unprovoked and dastardly assault which ought never to have been thought of much less inflicted.'[48] Edward was fined £3 plus costs of £1 13s. 6d. (or a month's hard labour in default).[49]

Edward's next – and as far as we know final – appearance in court occurred before Kidderminster County Petty Sessions in April 1911. It was as mundane a case as any in which he had been involved. But on this occasion it was he who took the initiative. He prosecuted two men who, he alleged, had stolen the collar from one of his dogs. Although the defendants denied the charge under oath, they were found guilty and imprisoned for seven days with hard labour.[50] It was a modest victory, an unprepossessing and unconvincing coda to Edward's years and years of legal wrangling.

Divorced, bankrupt and accused (though acquitted) of murder, Edward had moved to Kidderminster in the hope perhaps of distancing himself from the scenes of his disgrace, and regaining something at least of his former standing and respectability. If so, he did little to help himself. His legal battles with his ex-wife, his ex-father-in-law, his coal company, his architect and builders, his domestic staff and the local police force did his reputation no good at all. They meant that anybody who knew Edward, who read the papers – or spoke to somebody who did – would be exposed to a consistent and convincing view of him as irresponsible, violent and promiscuous, the absolute antithesis of late Victorian and Edwardian manly, middle-class respectability.

PART III

RESILIENCE

12

'I've plenty of money'[1]

COULD IT GET ANY WORSE for Edward? Divorced, bankrupt, accused of murder, pursued through the courts and struggling with a serious drink problem, he did nothing in Kidderminster to redeem, let alone enhance, his standing in the eyes of the local community. Indeed, if he was in any doubt as to the many failings to which he had fallen prey, he could read about many of them in the pages of his adopted town's newspapers.

Yet all was not lost. Edward's natural resilience reasserted itself, aided in no small measure by the fact that he remained surprisingly well off. His divorce, his bankruptcy, his prosecution for murder, his heavy drinking and his endless court appearances were inimical, of course, to all conventional notions of manliness, decency and respectability. But none of this prevented Edward from being recognised – and even respected – as a man of means. The recognition – and the respect – he received for the economic power he had at his disposal remained an unexpectedly powerful counterweight to everything that was undermining his respectability.

'In any case I am a bankrupt'[2]

Edward certainly remained comfortably off. The bankruptcy laws might or might not have been prime examples of nineteenth-century class legislation,[3] but there were ways around them, and Edward obviously knew – or learned – how to protect his assets. He prevaricated for years over the maintenance payments he was supposed to be making to Margaret and the children. He equivocated for nearly as long in his dealings with the official registrar. So although he knew perfectly well that bankrupts were required to declare all the property they possessed, he admitted failing to disclose both his shares in Wolverhampton racecourse and the deeds he owned to a property at the rear of his brewery.[4]

Not that the trustee in bankruptcy wished to leave Edward destitute. The trustee paid him, it seems, a lump sum of £1,000 together with an allowance of £6 a week.[5] Whatever the sources and the scale of his income, Edward was able live the final few years of his life in considerable comfort. Indeed, it may be no coincidence that he moved from Wolverhampton to Kidderminster in the summer of 1909, just before the bankruptcy proceedings against him were about to be instigated.

Whether or not the timing of the move was part of a plan to conceal his assets from future investigation, Edward appears to have used a third party to secure the property he was interested in buying. According to the Kidderminster press, it was a 'London gentleman', not a Wolverhampton brewer, who paid £1,100 for his new home, 'The Lea', an imposing five-bedroom house, set in two-and-half acres on high ground to the west of the town.[6] It was a substantial sum for a substantial house: the £1,100 that Edward paid for 'The Lea' would have been enough to buy him four 'villa residences' in the town, each with four bedrooms, a dining room, a drawing room and a 'good garden'.[7]

It was Edward, no 'London gentleman', who moved into The Lea, and Edward who began making improvements to it.[8] He did not do so on the cheap. He was able to employ both professionals to oversee the work and tradesmen to carry it out. We saw in the previous chapter that he hired an architect, Thomas Lowrie, to supervise the work, and engaged two builders, Richard Davies and Charles Walker, to undertake the repairs and alterations he wanted (at a cost of at least £200).[9]

Lowrie, Davies and Walker must have realised who was hiring them. Self-employed professionals and tradesmen made it their business, presumably, to keep their ears to the ground with regard to the credit-worthiness of potential clients. So why did they take the work? And why did they not walk away and cut their losses when the bankruptcy proceedings started? It could be that they did not care about – or were intrigued by – Edward's catastrophic fall from grace. It could be that they were persuaded by Edward's bearing and behaviour to believe that everything would turn out all right in the end. However, the most likely explanation is that they knew that people like Edward had ways and means of evading the more burdensome consequences of bankruptcy proceedings. Whatever their reasoning, they were prepared to draw a distinction between Edward's social standing and his economic power.

Certainly Edward made few concessions to his bankrupt status. Once installed in The Lea, he contrived to live very well indeed. He did not seem to have to work. Indeed, Fanny Thompson, the servant who took him to court, accused him of doing nothing but drink during the summer of 1910: 'You were in the drawing-room all day lying upon an easy chair with your face downwards, and it was not fit for a woman to be there.'[10]

He furnished the house comfortably and expensively. The hall, dining room, drawing room and morning rooms contained not just bookcases, oak tables and walnut and mahogany suites, but a pianola, 'valuable' oak and walnut sideboards, and 'two upright grand pianofortes'. Upstairs, the five bedrooms were furnished with bedsteads, chests of drawers and 'well made' suites of birch, walnut, and satin walnut. Outside in the house's extensive grounds, there were a stable and a coach house, an orchard and a kitchen garden, as well as two lawns for Edward and his friends to enjoy. In fact, when the house was sold after Edward's death, it contained, in addition to the furniture and effects listed above, 'plated goods', prints, etchings and oil paintings, eight cases of wine, and 'three hammerless and other guns'. It was such an important sale, announced the auctioneers charged with organising it, that it would take two full days to complete.[11]

Nor did Edward stint himself when it came to domestic help. The employment of servants, we have seen, was one of the key signifiers of middle-class (and sometimes upper working-class) status, distinguishing those able to afford such help from those below them in the economic and social scale.[12] Needless to say, Edward might well have had reasons other than class awareness – or a liking for good food and a clean home – for employing women about the house. But whatever his motives – and whatever their duties – what is striking is that Edward, though bankrupt and not working, was able to employ a series of servants after he moved from Wolverhampton to Kidderminster.

Despite Edward's reputation for drinking, violence and litigiousness, he did not seem to find it difficult to find women to work for him. We have met some of them already. When he moved to The Lea during the second half of 1909, he employed a Wolverhampton woman, Mrs Jane Peplow, as a 'sort of housekeeper'.[13] By August the following year, there was an eighteen- to twenty-year-old woman on the premises who, according to one of Kidderminster's court bailiffs, 'was dressed as servants are at a gentleman's house'.[14] A few weeks later, Fanny Thompson replaced Mrs Peplow as Edward's housekeeper. Fanny had placed an advertisement in the press, Edward had replied, and they agreed that she should work for him at a salary of £20 a year.[15] In the event, of course, she lasted barely four weeks. Fanny was replaced, in turn, by a general servant, Florence Timbrell, and two further housekeepers, Eleanor Beaton and May Austin.[16]

Bankrupt or not, working or not, it was no small matter to buy an £1,100 house, refurbish it, furnish it and staff it for several years with a succession of servants. But even these costs by no means exhausted the financial commitments which Edward entered into during his time in Kidderminster. At times The Lea must have seemed to be full of people, dogs and possibly visitors. Aside from his staff, he had his mistress, Emma Stacey, and a small, three- to four-year-old boy, presumably their illegitimate son, living with him during the second half of 1910.[17] He also kept at least two dogs, one of them a large bulldog, and employed a puddler, Henry Plant, to take them for walks.[18] Moreover, there was the suggestion, which Edward vehemently denied, that he used the 'huge fowl pen over 100 feet long and divided down the centre', which he had built in the garden, in order to indulge his interest in cock-fighting.[19]

As if these were not all burdens enough, Edward faced the costs attendant upon being a serial litigant. The problem was not so much that Edward lost many of the cases he fought, but that he often chose to be legally represented when fighting them. He managed in fact to delay or evade the financial consequences of many of the cases he lost. We have seen, for example, that although he owed Margaret considerable sums in maintenance, she found it exceptionally difficult to enforce her claims against him. He was never short of evasions and excuses. He appealed against the decisions of the court,[20] he questioned Margaret's behaviour, he said he needed to cross the cheque he had sent her.[21] He claimed he would have paid her if only he had known her address;[22] he claimed he would have paid her if only she had told him that she was in financial difficulties. 'I am prepared to make you a reasonable allowance for your maintenance,' he assured her. However, 'As you have made no application to me for money, I have taken it that you have not been in need of it.'[23]

Although he fought so many cases, and lost a good number of them, the penalties the courts imposed must often have seemed decidedly paltry to a man of his means. He was fined just 5s. plus costs for not having a collar on his dog,[24] and was ordered to pay the Cannock Chase Coal Company £3 2s. 6d. (and this for coal which he admitted having received).[25] He was instructed to pay less than £4 to the painter who had been working on his house,[26] and he was informed that he would have to pay into court the sum of £5 – another modest amount – if he wanted a new trial in his dispute with the builder Charles Walker.[27]

Even demands as modest as these provided Edward with opportunities for complaint and confrontation. He never tired of citing his bankruptcy.

When the judge at Kidderminster County Court told him he had decided in favour of the painter who had been working on his house, Edward had a ready, 'smiling' response: 'In any case I am a bankrupt.'[28] When the judge offered him a new trial in his dispute with Charles Walker if he paid the £5 into court, he retorted, 'Perhaps your Honour will please inform me how I am going to bring it into Court.' When his counsel reminded the court that his client was bankrupt, Edward was happy to confirm it: 'Absolutely I have nothing. Whatever the Trustee may have, I have nothing.' When Walker's counsel asked him if the trustee in bankruptcy was not making him an allowance of £6 a week, he replied sharply, 'You are wrongfully informed.' When the judge repeated that he needed to pay £5 into court if he wanted a new trial, Edward repeated the objection he had made before: 'Perhaps you will inform me where I can get it from.'[29]

The cost of fighting his cases was more of a problem. Although Edward sometimes represented himself in court, he usually engaged professionals to act on his behalf. They would be better equipped, he hoped, to dispute the maintenance he owed, to challenge the claims of his architect and builders – and to defend him against Councillor Smith's charge of assault. It could be an expensive business. When he failed to appear before Wolverhampton Bankruptcy Court in February 1910, he had his representative, Mr Haslam, hand the registrar a medical certificate to explain his absence. 'It is signed by Dr Addenbrooke,' explained Haslam. 'He is one of the best doctors in Kidderminster.'[30] When fighting some of his other cases, he engaged Smith Dorsett, the Birmingham barrister who had been a member of the legal team defending him at his trial for murder.[31] He did not come cheap. Smith Dorsett, recalled his former clerk, was 'one of the busiest men in the Midlands, no great lawyer, but a greater fighter, and much sought after for the defence in all criminal matters'.[32]

Despite Edward's bankruptcy, despite his lack of any visible means of support, and despite the fact that his spending seemed to continue largely unabated, Edward remained very comfortably off. When he died in August 1912, he left more than £2,750 in his will.[33] This was not a huge sum by the standards of the small minority of the population who died leaving property at the beginning of the twentieth century,[34] but it was a substantial amount for somebody who had faced the financial pressures that Edward had been under during the final years of his life.

'A gentleman's house'[35]

Those with money, it is often thought, can get away with almost anything. It is an adage to which Edward's final years lend a good deal of support. Edward's personal, financial and reputational resilience were mutually reinforcing, his fighting spirit and spending power transmogrifying, against all the odds, into an unexpected, residual respectability.

The economic resources that Edward had at his disposal meant, we have seen, that he was able to sustain a comfortable, middle-class standard of living. This meant, in turn, that those familiar with his disreputable past – and with his litigious tendencies – were inclined to treat him with a degree of caution. It is striking, for example, that when Edward first moved to Kidderminster, the local papers generally reported his difficulties and misdemeanours without any reference to what he had done, or what had happened to him, while he had been living in Wolverhampton.[36] It is more striking still that when the *Kidderminster Times* reported Edward's 1910 assault on Fanny Thompson, it did so under the headline, 'Extraordinary Allegations Against *A Gentleman*' (my italics).[37]

Edward's comfortable, middle-class standard of living also meant, apparently, that those coming across him for the first time were inclined to take him at face value. They assumed that he was what he seemed: a respectable, comfortably off, middle-aged, middle-class resident of one of the town's better districts. Court bailiffs, one imagines, were well used to distinguishing the deserving from the non-deserving, the respectable from the disreputable. Yet the Kidderminster county court bailiff who served a summons on Edward at The Lea in the summer of 1910 was in no doubt that he was dealing with a gentleman.

'Mr Gale, one of the bailiffs of the Court, said he served the summons by leaving it with a woman at Lawrence's house. She was apparently a servant, and was 18 or 20 years of age. He considered that she was a servant by her dress.'

'Did you ask if she was a servant?' demanded Edward's counsel.
'No.'
'Had she a cap on?'
'No.'
'Why did you think she was a servant?'
'By her dress. She was dressed as servants are at a gentleman's house.'[38]

Then, too, the fallen have attractions all of their own. The possibility of redemption was central, we know, to many late Victorians' and Edwardians' view of the world. This might be part at least of the reason that Edward's combination of insouciant disreputability and residual respectability proved irresistible both to some caring contemporaries and to certain representatives of the local media. Indeed, it was on this very point that Wolverhampton's *Midland Counties Express* chose to end the obituary of Edward which it published a day or two after his death.

> Lawrence, by his frequent appearances in local courts, attracted the attention of a local magistrate, who is well known for his zeal in religious and temperance work. This magistrate, hearing of Lawrence's illness, called upon him and found that he was in such a condition that he was not likely to recover. Very tactfully, therefore, he directed Lawrence's thoughts to spiritual questions, and from time to time he read the Scriptures by Lawrence's bedside, as did also the nurse who was in attendance upon him. Having regard to the past it must have been gratifying to both magistrate and nurse that Lawrence was very attentive to their ministrations.[39]

Edward died on 8 August 1912. Within a couple of days, the flag over Wolverhampton town hall was flying at half mast. It was a mark of respect: not, of course, for Edward, but for Sir Joseph Dimsdale, a man who epitomised everything that Edward was not. Educated at Eton, Dimsdale had become, *inter alia*, Master of the Grocers' Company, Grand Warden and Grand Treasurer of the Freemasons of England, Conservative MP for the City of London, Lord Mayor of London and – the reason the town hall flag was at half mast – an honorary freeman of Wolverhampton. The highlight of his career came, if *Who Was Who* is to be believed, when he 'carried the crystal sceptre of the City of London in front of His Majesty King Edward VII at his coronation'.[40] He was just the sort of man that respectable Wolverhampton liked to honour. Neither Sir Joseph Dimsdale nor Edward Lawrence was typical. But neither should be forgotten.

13

Gender, class and respectability

T HE *Express and Star* and the *Midland Counties Express* both reported Edward Lawrence's passing under the headline, 'Death of a Well-Known Wolverhampton Figure'.[1] It was a heading that reflected primarily, of course, the local perspective of two local newspapers.[2] But it also gives one pause for thought – or at least it does if one has spent three years of one's life writing the biography of a man whose life can be encapsulated in such casually dismissive fashion. One has to ask oneself whether it has been worth the time and effort involved in trying to rescue Edward Lawrence from the seeming contempt of his contemporaries and the virtual neglect of later generations.

The answer, I think, is yes. Edward Lawrence's life is interesting enough – and unusual enough – to be worth recording for its own sake. But Edward's life is also worth recording for what it tells us about late nineteenth- and early twentieth-century England – and for the questions it raises about the ways in which historians go about their business.

Edward and Ruth; biography and history

At one level, the book can be read as a who-done-it. Edward Lawrence killed Ruth Hadley, but was it an accident, was it manslaughter or was it murder? Did he have the motive, the means and the opportunity to kill her deliberately? Was there anything in their relationship to suggest that it was likely to end in recrimination, violence and death? The problem, if one can put it so tastelessly, is that there was – and there is – no smoking gun. Indeed, it is difficult to move beyond the prism of the trial. So much of what we know about Edward Lawrence, Ruth Hadley and their relationship derives, directly or indirectly, from what was revealed during Edward's arrest, prosecution and trial for her murder.

It is not easy to shake oneself free from this judicial embrace – and to remember all the time that one is dealing, not with facts and certainties, but with possibilities and probabilities. Nevertheless, the balance of probabilities is clear enough. Whatever reservations one may have with regard to the evidence produced during the course of the judicial process, it seems likely that the jury at Stafford Assizes reached the correct decision. The overwhelming likelihood is that Edward Lawrence killed Ruth Hadley during the course of a drunken argument that escalated out of control.[3]

The book can also be read, if one should wish to do so, as a morality tale. This is the story of a life – or rather several lives – that were ruined, according to one's view, by individual weakness, by unbridled promiscuity, by the easy availability of drink and/or by the unforgiving censoriousness of contemporary society. Each of these perspectives has its attractions, but each poses very considerable dangers. There is the risk, as always, of forcing the evidence to fit the argument. But this does not mean that we should shy away from attempting to explain, as well as to describe, how it was that Edward Lawrence came to kill Ruth Hadley in December 1908. It means rather that the lessons that one draws from the topic will depend, as ever, upon the beliefs and assumptions that one brings to bear upon it.

However, the book can be read most usefully as a contribution to the social, cultural, economic and even political history of late Victorian and Edwardian England. Edward's childhood, education and early career confirm and consolidate much of what we know about the domestic, business and political arrangements of middle-class families looking to make their way in the world. More striking still, Edward's return to Wolverhampton in the early 1890s opened up a Pandora's box of comment, assertion and innuendo that, used with care, reveals a good deal about the private and the public, the heterodox and the orthodox in turn-of-the-century provincial England.

The claim is not that Edward Lawrence was typical. He obviously was not. The claim is that it is his untypicality – and contemporaries' reactions to it – which makes him such an intriguing and informative subject for historical investigation. Edward lived an extraordinary life, a life that encourages us to look anew at three issues in particular: the supposed subordination and/or contented companionship of middle-class wives; the supposed powerlessness of working-class servants; and the supposed centrality-cum-fragility of middle-class respectability in Victorian and Edwardian England.

Marriage, service and respectability

Edward's relationship with Margaret does little to support commonly held notions about the balance of power in middle-class marriages. It points rather to the dangers of easy generalisation and, it is hoped, to the value of detailed studies such as this. It suggests that James Hammerton is correct in his view that gender relationships always tended to be a matter of dialogue and negotiation:

> We will more readily understand the complexities of marriage in the past by focusing on that dialogue, and on the various links between behaviour and discourse, rather than on the simple rise and fall of predominant models of marriage over the *longue durée*, which never tell more than a partial, often misleading story.[4]

Thus Edward's relationship with Margaret is less easy to characterise than it appears at first sight. As was pointed out in the opening chapter, it is obviously tempting to present Edward as a chauvinist bully, with Margaret his defenceless victim. But while there is not much doubt that Edward was a chauvinist bully, there is little doubt either that Margaret became less and less of a defenceless victim. She took legal action against her husband when he assaulted her; she sued him for divorce; and she pursued him through the courts for several years in her efforts to recover the maintenance she claimed he owed her.

Nor do Edward's household arrangements do much to sustain conventional notions about the vulnerability and passivity of those employed in domestic service. The women who worked for Edward were a good deal more confrontational than even recent, revisionist literature would lead one to suspect. Ruth Hadley and Emma Stacey manipulated the sexual and emotional relationships they had with their employer. Fanny Thompson appealed for police protection, and when this failed to deter Edward took out a summons against him for assault. Ruth Hadley, Kate Maddox, Elizabeth Wardle and Fanny Thompson all drew strength, it seems, from the kinship and neighbourhood ties embedded in working-class life. Ethel Cross, Kate Maddox and Elizabeth Wardle withdrew their labour in a way that was common in – and is often thought to be confined to – more industrialised sectors of the economy

However, Edward Lawrence's entire life can probably be read most helpfully as a commentary upon middle-class respectability: the means by which it was acquired, the forces that sustained and undermined it, and the difficulty with which it was dislodged. Edward's life confirms that respectability was a good deal more complicated than is generally thought.[5] Mike Huggins has been right therefore to try to dispel the tendency to regard respectability as a conveniently uncomplicated tool for examining social relationships during the late nineteenth and early twentieth centuries. This is what he and J.A. Mangan have to say on what they describe as 'a quicksilver phenomenon' in their introduction to the edited collection *Disreputable Pleasures: Less Virtuous Victorians at Play.*

> Respectability clearly was adapted to circumstances, occasions
> and events. The same actions could mean different things to
> different people in different places and at different time. The
> overriding conclusion to be drawn from *Disreputable Pleasures* is that
> "respectability" was a quicksilver phenomenon, reshaping itself to
> environment, gender, age and time.[6]

There is no doubt at all that Edward Lawrence's life provides a valuable test-bed on which to examine these, and other, claims about respectability – and disreputability – in Victorian and Edwardian England. But before it can be used in this way, certain caveats need to be entered. Edward was a man and different standards, it goes without saying, were applied by, and towards, men and women. Edward was middle-class, and different standards were applied too when it came to judging middle-class and working-class respectability. Edward and his family lived in the provinces, and provincial and metropolitan standards of what was acceptable could also differ very greatly. Then too, Edward and his father were businessmen, and entrepreneurial and professional standards of respectability differed, it will be suggested, more than those using the concept of respectability sometimes seem to recognise.

With these qualifications in mind, Edward Lawrence's life can be used, and used most helpfully, to explore respectability – and disreputability – during the late nineteenth and early twentieth centuries. When we examine Edward's life, we can see that we need to employ the term respectability with as much – and perhaps more – care and sensitivity as any other tool in the historian's conceptual armoury.

Edward's upbringing suggests that it was not necessarily as difficult as usually imagined for families like the Lawrences to attain the respectability they often craved. Even the Lawrences' modest beginnings, even their involvement in the drink trade, and even their own drinking, did not prevent them regarding themselves – and being regarded by some others at least – as respectable members of Wolverhampton society. Edward's adult years suggest too that even scandalously disreputable behaviour did not necessarily bring about the immediate social opprobrium one would have thought utterly inevitable.

It was the respectable, it has been said, who were best able to get away with disreputable behaviour. 'The flaunting of wealth,' suggest Simon Gunn and Rachel Bell, 'was acceptable so long as it was done with taste; the flouting of conventions was admissible so long as it was merely a flamboyant gesture, not a challenge to the accepted order of things.'[7] Thus men like Edward enjoyed a certain amount of leeway. Getting drunk, having a bet and behaving badly in front of the servants did not result automatically in loss of respectability. Indeed, contemporary perceptions of what did, and what did not, constitute acceptable behaviour ranged much more widely than we tend to imagine.[8]

Judge Howard Smith, it might be remembered, crossed swords with Edward in several courts, on several occasions. His education, upbringing and career were straightforwardly conventional: educated at St Paul's school, London and Trinity College, Cambridge, he was called to the bar in 1870, and served as recorder of Bridgnorth before becoming a county court judge in 1905.[9] However, Judge Smith's views as to what constituted acceptable and unacceptable behaviour were intriguingly contradictory. Sitting at Wolverhampton County Court in 1910, he railed against Edward for being 'drunken' and for having 'loose' 'relations with other women'.[10] However, sitting at West Bromwich County Court a few months later, he took it upon himself to defend gamblers (like Edward) and bookmakers from the criticism which was so often heaped upon them. 'A betting man is a gentleman as a rule, and does pay [his gambling debts]. Most bookmakers are respectable members of society, that is my experience; much better than the people who back with them.'[11]

Not many enjoyed the platforms that Judge Smith did to air their views. And none, so far as we know, came out openly in favour of what Edward got up to. But some at least of the local population were intrigued by Edward, the life he led, and the bizarre, sometimes life and death, situations in which he contrived to get himself involved. In Wolverhampton, it will be recalled, there was a rush for seats when Edward made his first appearance before the stipendiary magistrate, and he was the centre of attention when he was transferred from the police station to the railway station *en route* to Stafford Prison. And in Stafford, it will be remembered, the assizes was crowded when Edward's trial for murder began, and when it finished a large number of people gathered in the hope of seeing the man who had undergone 'such a terrible experience'.[12]

It was not just the disreputable who were tolerant of – or agnostic towards – disreputable behaviour. There was a substantial body of respectable opinion that believed in the possibility of redemption. The judge at Edward's trial for murder urged him to learn from his 'most terrible lesson'.[13] Edward's landlord in George Street thought he was guilty, but hoped his acquittal would 'be the means of him leading a better life'.[14] One of the magistrates who got to know Edward in Kidderminster called upon him during his final illness. 'Very tactfully, therefore, he directed Lawrence's thoughts to spiritual questions, and from time to time he read the scriptures by Lawrence's bedside.'[15]

Moreover, a substantial number of the middle-class, presumably respectable, residents of Wolverhampton and Kidderminster seemed to value economic success as highly as – or at least as well as – they did social propriety. They appeared to set particular store by entrepreneurial success, and to be prepared therefore to make allowances for the excesses in which risk-taking businessmen such as Joseph and Edward were prone perhaps to indulge.

Edward's father overcame the handicap of his modest background to establish a substantial and successful local business. When he died, he was described by no less a representative of mainstream values than the chief constable of Wolverhampton as 'a respectable and respected tradesman'.[16] Edward too benefited, it seems, from the tolerance and respect accorded to successful businessmen. The solicitors and barristers, the estate agents, the clerks and the tradesmen who worked for him were prepared to set aside whatever reservations they had concerning his character and behaviour in order to do business with him. Indeed, even after Edward's arrest for Ruth's murder, the chief constable was at pains to contrast his 'immoral conduct' and his commercial acumen. 'He has always been a shrewd and able man of business and I have never heard anything against him so far as the conduct of his business has been concerned.'[17]

Edward Lawrence was a man of his times. He was neither an exemplary citizen, an anonymous automaton, nor an extraordinary aberration. He was a recognisable, if unusual, example of a late Victorian and Edwardian, provincial, middle-class businessman whose life spiralled catastrophically out of control. It is not just the heroic, the worthy and the respectable who deserve our attention. So too do the ignoble, the disreputable and the despicable. So too do those, such as Edward Lawrence, who 'got into bad ways'.

Notes and references

Notes to Chapter 1: 'A terrible tragedy'

1. *Birmingham Gazette and Express*, 8 March 1909.
2. *Midland Counties Express*, 10 August 1912.
3. *Birmingham Gazette and Express*, 8 March 1909.
4. *Midland Counties Express*, 13 March 1909. There are two cursory accounts of the case: B. Roberts, *Murder in the Midlands* (Quercus: Warwick, 2000), pp. 97–9; and 'The Wolverhampton Merchant Accused of Murdering his Mistress – Saved from a Swinging by Britain's Most Brilliant Lawyer!', *Black Country Bugle*, 16 September 2004, p. 5. See also E. Marjoribanks, *The Life of Sir Edward Marshall Hall* (Gollancz, 1929), pp. 267–76.
5. *Times Law Reports*, 1908–9, xxv, p. 374.
6. National Archives (NA), J77/1, 859, 219856. See, for example, A. McLaren, *The Trials of Masculinity: Policing Sexual Boundaries, 1870–1930* (University of Chicago Press, 1997), p. 112. I owe this reference to Laura Ugolini.
7. *Midland Counties Express*, 19 January, 2 February 1907.
8. NA, A5516/44/4, 214971.
9. *Midland Evening News*, 8 December 1909; *Express and Star*, 29 April 1910.
10. *Kidderminster Shuttle*, 25 March 1911; *Kidderminster News*, 17 March, 25 August 1910; 26 March, 15 April 1911.
11. A. Marwick, *Nature of History* (Macmillan, 1989), p. 136.
12. J. Benson, *British Coalminers in the Nineteenth Century: A Social History* (Gill and Macmillan, 1989), ch. 7.
13. J. Benson, *The Rise of Consumer Society in Britain, 1880–1980* (Longman, 1994), ch. 3.
14. As proponents of microhistory suggest, small incidents, insignificant in themselves, can reveal a great deal about broader structures, attitudes and behaviour. See, for example, J.M. Bennett, 'Women's History: A Study in Continuity and Change', *Women's History Review*, 2, 1993, p. 177; V.A.C. Gatrell, *The Hanging Tree: Execution and the English People, 1770–1868* (Oxford University Press, 1996), p. 448; C. Steedman, *Master and Servant: Love and Labour in the English Industrial Age* (Cambridge University Press, 2007), p. 1.
15. S.G. Checkland, *The Rise of Industrial Society in England, 1815–1885* (Longman,

1964), pp. 318–19; G. Best, *Mid-Victorian Britain, 1851–70* (Fontana/Collins, 1979), p. 302; V.T.J. Arkell, *Britain Transformed: The Development of British Society since the Mid-Eighteenth Century* (Penguin, 1973), pp. 199–200.

16. One well-known example is C. Woodham-Smith, *Florence Nightingale, 1820–1910* (Constable, 1950).

17. See, for instance, M. Thomis and J. Grimmett, *Women in Protest, 1800–1850* (Croom Helm, 1982); M.L. Shanley, *Feminism, Marriage and the Law in Victorian England, 1850–1895* (Princeton University Press, 1989).

18. C. Hall, *White, Male and Middle Class: Explorations in Feminism and History* (Polity Press, 1992), p. 12; C. Smart, 'Introduction', in C. Smart (ed.), *Regulating Womanhood: Historical Essays on Marriage, Motherhood and Sexuality* (Routledge, 1992); A. Vickery, 'Golden Age to Separate Spheres? A Review of the Categories and Chronology of English Women's History', *Historical Journal*, 36, 1993; J. Tosh, 'What Should Historians do with Masculinity? Reflections on Nineteenth-Century Britain', *History Workshop Journal*, 38, 1994; M. Francis, 'The Domesticisation of the Male? Recent Research on Nineteenth- and Twentieth-Century British Masculinity', *Historical Journal*, 45, 2002.

19. L. Davidoff, *Worlds Between: Historical Perspectives on Gender and Class* (Polity Press, 1995), p. 9.

20. J. Tosh, 'Masculinities in an Industrialising Society: Britain, 1800–1914', *Journal of British Studies*, 44, 2005, p. 331. Also J. Tosh, 'Gentlemanly Politeness and Manly Simplicity in Victorian England', *Transactions of the Royal Historical Society*, 12, 2002.

21. A.J. Hammerton, *Cruelty and Companionship: Conflict in Nineteenth-Century Married Life* (Routledge, 1992), pp. 101, 114.

22. Hammerton, *Cruelty and Companionship*, p. 165. Also J. Tosh and J.A. Mangan (eds), *Manliness and Morality: Middle-Class Masculinity in Britain and America, 1800–1940* (Manchester University Press, 1987); M. Roper and J. Tosh (eds), *Manful Assertions: Masculinities in Britain since 1800* (Routledge, 1991); Tosh, 'Masculinities', p. 337.

23. See J. Benson, 'Domination, Subordination and Struggle: Middle-Class Marriage in Early Twentieth-Century Wolverhampton', *Women's History Review*, forthcoming.

24. See, for example, L. Davidoff Lockwood, 'Domestic Service and the Working-Class Life Cycle', *Bulletin of the Society for the Study of Labour History*, 26, 1973, pp. 10–11; P. Branca, *Silent Sisterhood: Middle Class Women in the Victorian Home* (Croom Helm), 1975, pp. 6–8; M. Ebery and B. Preston, *Domestic Service in Late Victorian and Edwardian England, 1871–1914* (University of Reading, 1976), p. 99; T.M. McBride, *The Domestic Revolution: The Modernisation of Household Service In England and France, 1820–1920* (Croom Helm, 1976), p. 9; E. Higgs, 'Domestic Servants and Households in Victorian England', *Social History*, 8, 1983, p. 202; E. Higgs, 'Domestic Service and Household Production', in A.V. John (ed.), *Unequal Opportunities: Women's Employment in England, 1800–1918* (Blackwell, 1986), p. 126. One master–servant relationship, that between A.J. Munby and Hannah Cullwick, looms enormously large in the literature: see L. Davidoff, 'Class and Gender in Victorian England: The Case of Hannah Cullwick and A.J. Munby', *Feminist Studies*, 5, 1979; L. Stanley, *The Auto/Biographical I: The Theory and Practice of Feminist Auto/Biography* (Manchester University Press, 1992), pp. 166–7; L. Davidoff, *Worlds Between*, pp. 111–12, 120.

25. J. Benson, *The Working Class in Britain, 1850–1939* (Longman, 1989), p. 24. See also E.O. Hellerstein, L.P. Hume and K.M. Offen (eds), *Victorian Women: A Documentary Account of Women's Lives in Nineteenth-Century England, France, and the United States* (Harvester Press, 1981), pp. 281–2; F.M.L. Thompson, *The Rise of Respectable Society: A Social History of Victorian Britain, 1830–1900* (Fontana, 1988); P. Horn, *The Rise and Fall of the Victorian Servant* (Alan Sutton, 1990), pp. 130–1; J. Burnett, *Useful Toil: Autobiographies of Working People from the 1820s to the 1920s* (Routledge, 1994), pp. 164–5; P. Bartley, *The Changing Role of Women 1815–1914* (Hodder & Stoughton, 1996), p. 53; L. Davidoff, M. Doolittle, J. Fink and K. Holden, *The Family Story: Blood, Contract and Intimacy 1830–1960* (Longman, 1999), pp. 165–70.

26. *Domestic Servants' Advertiser*, 20 May 1913; McBride, *Domestic Revolution*, p. 109. Horn, *Victorian Servant*, p. 125; P. Horn, *Life Below Stairs in the 20th Century* (Sutton Publishing, 2001), p. 10.

27. Horn, *Life Below Stairs*, p. 8. Also Thompson, *Respectable Society*, pp. 248–9.

28. Davidoff, *et al.*, *Family Story*, p. 171. Also Davidoff, 'Domestic Service', 11, 13; Davidoff, *Worlds Between*, pp. 26–8; McBride, *Domestic Revolution*, p. 99.

29. See J. Benson, 'One Man and his Women: Domestic Service in Edwardian England', *Labour History Review*, 72, 2007.

30. For example, P. Thompson, *The Edwardians: The Remaking of British Society* (Paladin, 1977), p. 302; P. Bailey, *Leisure and Class in Victorian England: Rational Recreation and the Contest for Control, 1830–1885* (Methuen, 1978), pp. 182–5; Best, *Mid-Victorian Britain*, pp. 282–6; Thompson, *Respectable Society*, pp. 173–4.

31. Best, *Mid-Victorian Britain*, p. 284.

32. M.J. Huggins, 'More Sinful Pleasures?: Leisure, Respectability and the Male Middle Classes in Victorian England', *Journal of Social History*, Spring, 2000, p. 585. Also M. Huggins, 'Culture, Class and Respectability: Racing and the English Middle Classes in the Nineteenth Century', *International Journal of the History of Sport*, 11, 1994, p. 26; M. Huggins, *Flat Racing and British Society, 1790–1914: A Social and Economic History* (Cass, 2000), pp. 4–5; M. Huggins and J.A. Mangan, 'Prologue: All Mere Complexities', in M. Huggins and J.A. Mangan (eds), *Disreputable Pleasures: Less Virtuous Victorians at Play* (Cass, 2004), p. xx.

33. Thompson, *Respectable Society*.

34. S. Gunn and R. Bell, *Middle Classes: Their Rise and Sprawl* (Cassell, 2002), p. 49.

35. See J. Benson, 'Drink, Death and Bankruptcy: Retailing and Respectability in Late Victorian and Edwardian England', *Midland History*, xxxii, 2007.

Notes to Chapter 2: Family history and antecedents

1. NA, A5516/44/4, 214971, Copy/Police Report as to prisoner's antecedents, L.R. Burnett to Director of Public Prosecutions, 29 January 1908 [1909].

2. N. Williams, *Chronology of the Modern World* (Penguin, 1975), pp. 270–5; M. Pugh, *The Making of Modern British Politics 1867–1939* (Blackwell, 1982), p. 5.

3. *Midland Evening News*, 2 December 1901.

4. D.M. Palliser, *The Staffordshire Landscape* (Hodder & Stoughton, 1976), p. 167.

5. R.H. Trainor, *Black Country Elites: The Exercise of Authority in an Industrialized Area, 1830–1900* (Clarendon Press, 1993), p. 23.

6. *White's Directory of Birmingham*, 1869, pp. 780–3; G.J. Barnsby, *Social Conditions in*

the Black Country, 1800–1900 (Integrated Publishing Services: Wolverhampton, 1980), Table 1; Palliser, *Staffordshire Landscape*, pp. 187–8.

7. Trainor, *Black Country Elites*, p.8.

8. K.H. Hawkins and C.L. Pass, *The Brewing Industry: A Study in Industrial Organisation and Public Policy* (Heinemann, 1979), pp. 16–18; J. Benson, *The Penny Capitalists: A Study of Nineteenth-Century Working-Class Entrepreneurs* (Gill and Macmillan, 1984), pp. 114–27; B. Harrison, *Drink and the Victorians: The Temperance Question in England, 1815–1872* (Keele University Press, 1994), pp. 309–34.

9. J.M. Goldstrom (ed.), *The Working Classes in the Victorian Age, Volume III, Urban Conditions, 1848–1868* (Gregg International, 1973), p. 433.

10. Information from Bill Piggins.

11. *White's Directory of Birmingham*, 1869, p. 754.

12. *White's Birmingham Directory*, 1873, p. 1843. See G. Shaw (ed.), *Directing the Past: Directories and the Local Historian* (Local Historian, 2003).

13. Hawkins and Pass, *Brewing Industry*, pp. 27–8.

14. *Hulley's Hardware District Directory*, 1889–90, p. 44; *Kelly's Directory of Staffordshire*, 1894, p. 10; *Kelly's Directory of Birmingham*, 1903, p. 150; High Court of Justice, Probate Registry, Lichfield, 05/01/0295, 21 February 1902.

15. *Midland Evening News*, 2 December 1901.

16. *National Probate Calendar*, 1902, p. 85.

17. *Wolverhampton Red Book*, 1901, p. 27.

18. H. Perkin, *The Rise of Professional Society: England since 1880* (Routledge, 1989), p. 78.

19. Barnsby, *Social Conditions*, pp. 209–10; G.J. Barnsby, *A History of Housing in Wolverhampton, 1750–1975* (Integrated Publishing Services: Wolverhampton, 1976?), p. 45.

20. *Birmingham Gazette and Express*, 5 March 1909, Inspector Hill.

21. P. Jelland, *Death in the Victorian Family* (Oxford University Press, 1996), p. 252. Also J.R. Gillis, *For Better, For Worse: British Marriages, 1600 to the Present* (Oxford University Press, 1985), p. 110; C. D. J. Pearsall, 'Burying the Duke: Victorian Mourning and the Funeral of the Duke of Wellington', *Victorian Literature and Culture*, 1999.

22. *Licensed Victuallers' Gazette*, 1 May 1880.

23. *Licensed Victuallers' Gazette*, 10 January 1880. Also 10 July 1880, 8 January 1909.

24. *White's Directory of Birmingham*, 1869, p. 754; A. Brew, *Wolverhampton Pubs* (Tempus: Stroud, 2004), p. 76.

25. *Census of England and Wales*, 1881.

26. *Midland Counties Express*, 31 October 1891. Also *Licensed Victuallers' Gazette*, 24 July 1891.

27. P. Jennings, *The Public House in Bradford, 1770–1970* (Keele University Press, 1995), p. 47.

28. The reported cause of death was 'double pneumonia'. See Wolverhampton Registration District, HD 074787, Death Certificate. Also *Birmingham Gazette and Express*, 5 March 1909, Inspector Hill; *Midland Counties Express*, 6 March 1909, Marshall Hall.

29. *Birmingham Gazette and Express*, 5 March 1909. Also *Staffordshire Advertiser*, 6 March 1909.

30. *Birmingham Gazette and Express*, 5 March 1909.
31. L.R. Burnett to Director of Public Prosecutions, 29 January 1908 [1909].
32. Probate Registry, 21 February 1902. See also Wolverhampton Archives (WA), D-NAJ/A/7/3, Boswell & Tomlins.
33. *Kelly's Directory of Staffordshire*, 1892, p. 449.
34. *Census of England and* Wales, 1891; *Wolverhampton Red Books*, *passim*; L. Davidoff, M. Doolittle, J. Fink and K. Holden, *The Family Story: Blood, Contract and Intimacy, 1830–1960* (Longman, 1999), p. 162. Also N. Judson, 'Domestic Servants in Wolverhampton 1871–901', unpublished MA dissertation (University of Wolverhampton, 2006).
35. United Grand Lodge of England, Freemasons' Hall, London, Dartmouth Lodge, West Bromwich, Membership Register, 1863–87; List of Contributing Members, 1902; *Bye-Laws of the Dartmouth Lodge of Ancient Free & Accepted Masons, No. 662, West Bromwich*, 1890, pp. 15–19.
36. R. Burt, 'Freemasonry and Business Networking during the Victorian Period', *Economic History Review*, lvi, 2003, p. 666.
37. *Midland Evening News*, 2 December 1901.
38. D. Gardiner, 'The Nature and Development of Conservatism in Wolverhampton 1886–1910', unpublished MA dissertation (University of Wolverhampton, 1991), p. 34. See also *Licensed Victuallers' Gazette*, 13, 27 March 1880.
39. *Midland Counties Express*, 31 October 1891.
40. J. Lawrence, 'Class and Gender in the Making of Urban Toryism, 1880–1914', *English Historical Review*, 108, 1993, p. 639.
41. *Midland Counties Express*, 7 January 1901.
42. Lawrence, 'Class and Gender', p. 650.
43. P.M. Young, *Centenary Wolves* (Wolverhampton Wanderers F.C., 1976), p. 57.
44. Lawrence, 'Class and Gender', pp. 640–41.
45. Cited in T. Mason, *Association Football and English Society, 1863–1915* (Harvester Press), 1981, p. 48.
46. *Midland Evening News*, 2 December 1901; www.medicine.bham.ac.uk/histmed_school.htm
47. *Midland Evening News*, 5 December 1901.
48. *Midland Counties Express*, 7 December 1901.
49. L.R. Burnett to Director of Public Prosecutions, 29 January 1908 [1909].

Notes to Chapter 3: 'A sound English education'

1. *Post Office Directory of Bath*, 1886/7, p. x.
2. P. Jennings, *The Public House in Bradford, 1770–1970* (Keele University Press, 1995), p. 127.
3. *Birmingham Gazette and Express*, 5 March 1909, Inspector Hill; *Midland Counties Express*, 6 March 1909, Marshall Hall.
4. C. Hall, *White, Male and Middle Class: Explorations in Feminism and History* (Polity Press, 1992), ch. 4.
5. Merridale Cemetery, Wolverhampton, Joseph Lawrence tombstone; *Census of England and Wales*, 1871, 1881, 1891, 1901. Cf. J. Snarey, *How Fathers Care for the Next Generation: A Four-Decade Study* (Harvard University Press, 1993).
6. *Census of England and Wales*, 1871, 1891.

7. F.M.L. Thompson, *The Rise of Respectable Society: A Social History of Victorian Britain, 1830–1900* (Fontana, 1988), p. 197.

8. E. Roberts, *Women's Work, 1840–1940* (Cambridge University Press, 1988), p. 19.

9. *Census of England and Wales*, 1871.

10. L. Davidoff, M. Little, J. Fink and K. Holden, *The Family Story: Blood, Contract and Intimacy 1830–1960* (Longman, 1999), pp. 158–9.

11. *Kelly's Directory of Warwickshire*, 1880, p. 791.

12. *Census of England and Wales*, 1881, RG11, 3021/130, p. 21.

13. K.S. Inglis, *Churches and the Working Classes in Victorian England* (Routledge and Kegan Paul, 1963), p. 24.

14. *Post Office Bath Directory, 1884–85*, pp. 606–15; *Bath Herald*, 16 July, 27 August 1881; 2 September 1882; C. Ball, *The History of a Parish: St John the Evangelist Lower Weston Bath* (Bath, 1986?), p. 9; J. Hargood-Ash, *Two Thousand Years in the Life of a Somerset Village, Weston, Bath* (Weston Local History Society, 2001).

15. F. Musgrove, 'Middle-Class Education and Employment in the Nineteenth Century', *Economic History Review*, xii, 1959–60, p. 102.

16. *Census of England and Wales*, RG11/2443, 34–39.

17. See 'IGNORANCE' to *Bath Herald*, 11 August 1882; 'PLANTAGENET DE JONES' to *Bath Herald*, 14 August 1882; *Post Office Bath Directory 1884–85*, p. 613.

18. *Post Office Directory of Bath*, 1886/7, p. x.

19. *Post Office Directory of Bath*, 1886/7, p. x. See also *Bath Herald*, 26 August 1882.

20. www.staffs.ac.uk/schools/humanities_and_soc_sciences/pgstudents/rugby/blanc   ... 23/9;2005

21. R. Holt, *Sport and the British: A Modern History* (Oxford University Press, 1990), pp. 82–3. Also P. Bailey, *Leisure and Class in Victorian England: Rational Recreation and the Contest for Control, 1830–1885* (Methuen, 1987), pp. 86, 136.

22. *Bath Herald*, 24 July, 18 September 1882; www.staffs.ac.uk/schools/humanities

23. *Bath Herald*, 23 July 1881. Also 22 July 1882.

24. These events were similar to those organised at militia sports. See, for example, *Scottish Leader*, 11 July 1887.

25. *Bath Herald*, 6 July 1881.

26. Holt, *Sport and the British*, p. 90. Also J. Tosh, 'Masculinities in an Industrialising Society: Britain, 1800–1914', *Journal of British Studies*, 44, 2005, pp. 332–3.

Notes to Chapter 4: Member of the Royal College of Veterinary Surgeons

1. *Midland Counties Express*, 6 March 1909.

2. J.R. Fisher, 'Not Quite a Profession: The Aspirations of Veterinary Surgeons in England in the Mid Nineteenth Century', *Historical Research*, 66, 1993. See also I. Pattison, *The British Veterinary Profession, 1791–1948* (Allen, 1984), chs 9–10; H. Perkin, *The Rise of Professional Society: England since 1800* (Routledge, 1989), p. 85.

3. *Veterinary Record*, 19 October 1889.

4. Fisher, 'Profession', pp. 287–8.

5. *Veterinary Record*, 29 September 1888. Also 10 May, 28 June 1890.

6. B. Rutherford, 'Veterinary Education', *Veterinary Record*, 28 November 1891.

7. *Veterinary Record*, 4 August 1888.

8. Information from Frances Houston.

9. For example, I.H. Adams, *The Making of Urban Scotland* (Croom Helm, 1978), chs 7–8.

10. *Scottish Leader*, 31 January, 2 March 1887.

11. *Veterinary Record*, 9 August 1890; O.C. Bradley, *History of the Edinburgh Veterinary College*, 1923 (reprinted Edinburgh University Library, 1988), pp. 65–6; S.A. Hall, 'John Gamgee and the Edinburgh New Veterinary College', *Veterinary Record*, 16 October 1965.

12. *Scottish Leader*, 10 March 1887.

13. *Scottish Leader*, 3 February 1887. See also 8 January 1887.

14. *Scottish Leader*, 1 February 1887.

15. *Edinburgh Evening News*, 15, 17 January 1887; Bradley, *Edinburgh Veterinary College*, pp. 72–3.

16. *Edinburgh Evening News*, 18 January, 11, 14 April, 3 May 1887; 'HOME RULE' to *Scottish Leader*, 22 February 1887; *Scottish Leader*, 15 January 1887; *Scottish Leader*, 12, 15 April 1887.

17. *Scottish Leader*, 2, 4 April 1887, and *passim*.

18. *Scottish Leader*, 16 February 1887.

19. 'M.R.C.V.S.' to *Scottish Leader*, 15 February 1887.

20. *Scottish Leader*, 12 April 1887.

21. *Veterinary Record*, 18 October 1890. See also 12, 26 April 1890.

22. *Slater's Directory of Edinburgh and Leith*, 1889, p. 12; A.A. Macdonald, C.M. Warwick and W.T. Johnson, 'Locating Veterinary Education in Edinburgh in the Nineteenth Century', *Book of the Old Edinburgh Club*, 6, 2005, p. 61. For the curriculum, see University of Liverpool, Special Collections and Archives, D492, J.Rigby papers.

23. J. M'Fadyean to *Scottish Leader*, 5 February 1887.

24. *The Register of Veterinary Surgeons*, 1886, pp. 48–50.

25. Royal College of Veterinary Surgeons, London, 'Dead Members' file; *Veterinary Record*, 16 February 1889; *Register of Veterinary Surgeons*, 1888–1911.

26. *Scottish Leader*, 12 April 1887; *Veterinary Record*, 4 August, 8 September 1888.

27. See *Veterinary Record*, 28 June 1890, and J.Ware and H. Hunt, *The Several Lives of a Victorian Vet* (Bachman and Turner, 1979), a fascinating account, *inter alia*, of practice in Bridgnorth in the late 1850s.

28. *Veterinary Record*, 12 January 1889.

29. See *Newport and Market Drayton Advertiser*, 17 September 1887; *Porter's Directory of Salop*, 1888, pp. 459–61; *Midland Counties Express*, 6 March 1909.

30. Shifnal Public Library, unpublished dissertation, ND, p. 20.

31. Edward Lawrence's business card, ND. I am grateful to Bill Piggins for showing this to me.

32. *Wellington Standard*, 1 March 1888.

33. *Wellington Standard*, 22 November 1888. Also *Newport and Market Drayton Advertiser*, 24 November 1888.

34. *Veterinary Record*, 23 August 1890. Also 'One of the Crowd' to *Veterinary Record*, 26 September 1891; *Veterinary Record*, 17 October 1891.

35. H. Gray to *Veterinary Record*, 8 September 1888.

36. *Slater's Directory of Shropshire and Wales*, 1868, p. 76.

37. *Newport and Market Drayton Advertiser*, 25 August, 15 September 1888; *Wellington*

Standard, 11 July, 10 December 1889.

38. *Veterinary Record*, 29 September 1888; *Wolverhampton Red Book*, 1901, p. 27. Also A. Hardy, 'Professional Advantage and Public Health: British Veterinarians and State Veterinary Services, 1865–1939', *Twentieth Century British History*, 14, 1, 2003, p. 9.

39. *Porter's Directory of Salop*, 1888, pp. 457–9.

40. *Veterinary Record*, 2 January 1909.

41. *The Times*, 8 March 1909.

42. *Porter's Directory of Salop*, 1888, p. 454.

43. *Newport and Market Drayton Advertiser*, 29 September 1888; *Wellington Standard*, 7 March 1889.

44. *Newport and Market Drayton Advertiser*, 23 April 1887; *Wellington Standard*, 24 May, 12 July, 26 July 1888.

45. Tosh, 'Masculinities', pp. 339, 341. Also J. Tosh, *A Man's Place: Masculinity and the Middle Class Home in Victorian England* (Yale University Press, 1999), ch. 4.

46. *Licensed Victuallers' Gazette*, 15 August 1902.

47. Cited in *Wellington Standard*, 16 May 1889.

48. *Veterinary Record*, 7 December 1889.

49. *Veterinary Record*, 18 May 1889. The Buenos Ayres *Standard* carried advertisements by two practices between 1889 and 1891. See *Standard, passim*.

50. *Veterinary Record*, 29 September 1888.

51. *Staffordshire Advertiser*, 6 March 1909; *Staffordshire Chronicle*, 6 March 1909. Despite extensive efforts in Argentina, no trace has been found of Edward's time in the country.

52. *Standard*, 12 January 1889; 11 February, 17 May 1890.

53. *Midland Counties Express*, 6 March 1909. See, for example, R. Hora, *The Landowners of the Argentine Pampas: A Social and Political History* (Clarendon Press, 2001), ch. 2.

54. D.C.M. Platt, *Latin America and British Trade 1806–1914* (Black, 1972), p. 130.

55. Platt, *Latin America*, p. 19; information from Paul Henderson;

56. *Standard*, 14 January, 30 March 1890 and *passim*.

57. *Standard*, 15 May 1890; Platt, *Latin America*, pp. 104–5; F. Capie, 'The Emergence of the Bank of England as a Mature Central Bank', in D. Winch and P O'Brien (eds), *The Political Economy of British Historical Experience, 1688–1914* (Oxford University Press, 2002), p. 307.

58. *Standard*, 15 May 1890.

59. *Court Guide and County Blue Book of Warwickshire, Worcestershire and Staffordshire* (Deacon, 1902), p. 718.

60. *The Register of Veterinary Surgeons, passim*.

Notes to Chapter 5: 'Married a respectable person'

1. NA, A5516/44/4, 214971, Copy/Police Report as to prisoner's antecedents, L.R. Burnett to Director of Public Prosecutions, 29 January 1908 [1909].

2. *Midland Counties Express*, 6 March 1909.

3. *Staffordshire Advertiser*, 6 March 1909.

4. E. Marjoribanks, *The Life of Sir Edward Marshall Hall* (Gollancz, 1929), p. 268.

5. WA, T-MAG/5/3, 'Alehouses, Register of Licences', 1892+.

6. High Court of Justice, Probate Registry, Lichfield, 05/01/0295, 21 February 1902.

7. L.R. Burnett to Director of Public Prosecutions, 29 January 1908 [1909].

8. L. Davidoff, M. Doolittle, J. Fink and K. Holden, *The Family Story: Blood, Contract and Intimacy 1830–1960* (Longman, 1999), pp. 125–6.

9. Wolverhampton Registration District, AA878679, Marriage Certificate, 7 February 1893.

10. L.R. Burnett to Director of Public Prosecutions, 29 January 1908 [1909].

11. Marriage Certificate, 7 February 1893.

12. J.R. Gillis, *For better, For Worse: British Marriages, 1600 to the Present* (Oxford University Press, 1985), p. 235.

13. NA, J77/1, 859, 219856, High Court of Justice, Probate, Divorce, and Admiralty Division, Lawrence *v.* Lawrence, Court Minutes, Petition, 3 October 1905.

14. *Midland Counties Express*, 6 March 1909, Edward Lawrence.

15. Divorce Petition, 3 October 1905. A.J. Hammerton, *Cruelty and Companionship: Conflict in Nineteenth-Century Married Life* (Routledge, 1992), part II.

16. Hammerton, *Cruelty and Companionship*, pp. 101, 114.

17. Divorce Petition, 3 October 1905.

18. *Census of England and Wales*, 1901, RG13, 2678, 82.

19. P. Bartley, *Prostitution: Prevention and Reform in England, 1860–1914* (Routledge, 2000), p. 7; P. Horn, *The Rise and Fall of the Victorian Servant* (Alan Sutton, 1990), ch. 7.

20. Davidoff *et al.*, *The Family Story*, p. 177.

21. *Midland Counties Express*, 6 March 1909.

22. *Midland Counties Express*, 6 March 1909.

23. L.R. Burnett to Director of Public Prosecutions, 29 January 1908 [1909].

24. *Midland Counties Express*, 6 March 1909, Edward Lawrence.

25. WA, D-NAJ/A/7/3, Nock & Joseland, E. Lawrence to Nock & Joseland, 21 December 1908; *Midland Counties* Express, 11 October 1907.

26. *Staffordshire Advertiser*, 6 March 1909.

27. L.R. Burnett to Director of Public Prosecutions, 29 January 1908 [1909].

Notes to Chapter 6: 'Up to his games again'

1. *Midland Counties Express*, 6 March 1909.

2. T. Boliver, *South Staffordshire Golf Club 1892–1992* (South Staffordshire Golf Club: Wolverhampton, 1992), pp. 3–9.

3. C. Upton, *A History of Wolverhampton* (Phillimore, 1998), p. 94.

4. Cited in D. Clayton, *Wolverhampton's Empire Palace of Varieties 1898–1921* (D.B.C. Enterprise: Wolverhampton), p. 5.

5. Upton, *Wolverhampton*, pp. 101–2; M.B. Rowlands, *The West Midlands from AD 1000* (Longman, 1987), p. 328.

6. J. Lawrence, 'Popular Politics and the Limitations of Party: Wolverhampton, 1867–1900', in E.F. Biagini and A.J. Reid (eds), *Currents of Radicalism: Popular Radicalism, Organised Labour And Party Politics in Britain, 1850–1914* (Cambridge University Press, 1991), p. 75.

7. For example, *Sporting Chronicle*, 7, 13, 19 March 1900; 27 April 1901.

8. J. Pinfold, 'Dandy Rats at Play: The Liverpudlian Middle Classes and Horse-Racing in the Nineteenth Century', in M. Huggins (ed.), *Disreputable Pleasures: Less Virtuous*

Victorians at Play (Cass, 2004); M. Huggins, 'Betting and Gambling', unpublished paper (n.d.). I am very grateful to Mike Huggins for allowing me to have access to this work.

9. *Sporting Chronicle*, 7 May 1901; *Midland Counties Express*, 6 March 1909; *Birmingham Gazette and Express*, 5 March 1909.

10. Bankruptcy statement, 1910.

11. M. Huggins, *Flat Racing and British Society 1790–1914: A Social and Economic History* (Cass, 2000), p. 77.

12. Huggins, *Flat Racing*, pp. 117, 138.

13. *Licensed Victuallers' Gazette*, 30 January 1891.

14. Upton, *Wolverhampton*, p. 103. Also *Licensed Victuallers' Gazette*, 2 January 1891, 26 December 1902, 18 January 1905.

15. *Wolverhampton Chronicle*, 6 January 1909.

16. J.R. Burnett to Director of Public Prosecutions, 29 January 1908 [1909].

17. For example, D. Kirby, *Barmaids: A History of Women's Works in Pubs* (Cambridge University Press, 1998), p. 4.

18. *Licensed Victuallers' Gazette*, 3 January 1902.

19. *Licensed Victuallers' Gazette*, 25 April 1902.

20. *Newport and Market Drayton Advertiser*, 10 December 1887.

21. Bartley, *Prostitution*, p. 6.

22. Interview with Mrs A, daughter of Kate Maddox, 14 July 2005.

23. GRO, Births, March Quarter 1873, Folio 6H, p. 630?

24. Interview with Mr A, grandson of Ruth Hadley's uncle, 3 June 2005.

25. *Licensed Victuallers' Gazette*, 8 January 1909.

26. E. Marjoribanks, *The Life of Sir Edward Marshall Hall* (Gollancz, 1929), p. 268.

27. *Census*, 1901, RG 13, 2681, 14, 19, 121.

28. *Midland Counties Express*, 6 March 1909.

29. Interview with Mrs A.

30. *Midland Counties Express*, 6 March 1909.

31. *Midland Counties Express*, 6 March 1909.

32. *Wolverhampton Chronicle*, 6 January 1909.

33. *Midland Counties Express*, 6 March 1909.

34. Court Minutes, Petition, 3 October 1905.

35. Court Minutes, Petition, 3 October 1905.

36. *Midland Counties Express*, 6 March 1909.

37. *Birmingham Gazette and Express*, 5 March 1909; *Midland Counties Express*, 6 March 1909.

38. Wolverhampton Registration District, CN357016; *Midland Counties Express*, 6 March 1909.

39. Interview with Mrs B, great niece of Ruth Hadley, 1 November 2005; *Times Law Reports*, xxv, 1908–9, p. 374; *Staffordshire Chronicle*, 6 March 1909.

40. Court Minutes, Petition, 3 October 1905.

41. Court Minutes, Petition, 3 October 1905.

42. *Express and Star*, 28 July 1905; Court Minutes, Petition, 3 October 1905.

43. M.J. Wiener, 'The Sad Story of George Hall: Adultery, Murder and the Politics of Mercy In Mid-Victorian England', *Social History*, 24, 1999, p. 185; G. Frost, '"She is but a Woman": Kitty Bryan and the English Edwardian Criminal Justice System',

Gender & History, 16, 2004, pp. 547, 552. Also A. McLaren, *The Trials of Masculinity: Policing Sexual Boundaries 1870–1930* (University of Chicago Press, 1997), ch.5.

44. See A.J. Hammerton, 'Victorian Marriage and the Law of Matrimonial Cruelty', *Victorian Studies*, 33, 1990, pp. 286–7.

45. *Express and Star*, 28 July 1905.

46. D. Coleman, 'Population and Family' in A.H. Halsey with J. Webb (eds), *Twentieth-Century British Social Trends* (Macmillan, 2000), p. 62.

47. M.L. Shanley, '"One Must Ride Behind": Married Women's Rights and the Divorce Act of 1857', *Victorian Studies*, 25, 1982; Hammerton, 'Victorian Marriage', p. 271; G. Savage, '"The Wilful Communication of a Loathsome Disease: Marital Conflict and Venereal Disease in Victorian England', *Victorian Studies*, 34, 1990, p. 38.

48. *Midland Counties Express*, 6 March 1909. Also *Birmingham Gazette and Express*, 5 March 1909.

49. *Midland Counties Express*, 6 March 1909.

50. *Midland Counties Express*, 6 March 1909. Also *Birmingham Gazette and Express*, 5 March 1909.

51. *Midland Counties Express*, 6 March 1909. Also *Birmingham Gazette and Express*, 5 March 1909.

52. *Staffordshire Advertiser*, 6 March 1909.

53. Court Minutes; *Midland Counties Express*, 6 March 1909, Edward Lawrence.

Notes to Chapter 7: 'Addicted to drink'

1. *Midland Evening News*, 11 October 1907.

2. *Kelly's Directory of Staffordshire*, 1905, pp. 576, 699; *Midland Counties Express*, 19 January 1907. See J. McKenna, *Black Country Breweries* (Tempus: Stroud, 2005), ch. 2.

3. *Express and Star*, 11 October 1907; *Midland Counties Express*, 6 March 1909.

4. NA, A5516/44/4, Copy/Police Report as to prisoner's antecedents, F. Williams deposition.

5. *Midland Counties Express*, 19 January 1907; *Kelly's Directory of Worcestershire*, 1908, p. 208. Margaret had also moved to Oldbury after leaving Edward.

6. *Midland Counties Express*, 19 January 1907; 6 March 1909.

7. *Midland Counties Express*, 6 March 1909.

8. J. Benson, *The Working Class in Britain, 1850–1939* (Longman, 1989), ch. 5. Also E. Roberts, *A Woman's Place: An Oral History of Working-Class Women 1890–1940* (Blackwell, 1984), ch. 5.

9. Copy/Police Report as to prisoner's antecedents, F. Williams deposition.

10. *Express and Star*, 29 January 1907; *Midland Counties Express*, 2 February 1907.

11. *Midland Counties Express*, 19 January 1907.

12. *Midland Counties Express*, 19 January 1907.

13. *Midland Counties Express*, 19 January 1907.

14. *Midland Counties Express*, 19 January 1907.

15. *Midland Counties Express*, 2 February 1907.

16. *Express and Star*, 15 January 1907; *Midland Counties Express*, 19 January 1907.

17. *Express and* Star, 29 January 1907; *Midland Counties Express*, 2 February 1907.

18. *Express and Star*, 29 January 1907. Also *Midland Counties Express*, 2 February 1907.
19. *Express and Star*, 11 October 1907.
20. *Midland Counties Express*, 6 March 1909.
21. *Midland Counties Express*, 6 March 1909.
22. For full details of the charges, see WA, T-QS/A/1/8, Borough of Wolverhampton Record Book, No. 8, General Quarter Sessions, 11 October 1907.
23. *Midland Evening News*, 11 October 1907. The remainder of the case was much less newsworthy: the accused clerk gave evidence, and the proceedings concluded with the defence calling two character witnesses to speak on their client's behalf.
24. *Express and Star*, 11 October 1907. Also *Midland Evening News*, 11 October 1907.
25. Copy/Police Report as to prisoner's antecedents, L.R. Burnett to Director of Public Prosecutions, 29 January 1908 [1909].
26. Information from Bill Piggins.
27. A.E. Bowker, *Behind the Bar* (Staples Press, 1947), p. 30.
28. Copy/Police Report as to prisoner's antecedents, L.R. Burnett to Director of Public Prosecutions, 29 January 1908 [1909].
29. P. Thompson, *The Edwardians: The Remaking of British Society* (Paladin, 1977), p. 89.
30. D. Coleman, 'Population and Family', in A.H. Halsey with J. Webb (eds), *Twentieth-Century British Social Trends* (Macmillan, 2000), p. 62.
31. *Wolverhampton Record Book* (n.p., 1901), p. 75; The *Wulfrunian*, April 1908, p. 117; *Wolverhampton Grammar School Register 1515-1920* (Titus Wilson, 1926?), p. 200.
32. Interview with Mrs A.
33. *Wolverhampton Grammar School Register*, p. 346.
34. *Staffordshire Advertiser*, 6 March 1909.
35. *Midland Counties Express*, 6 March 1909.
36. *Midland Counties Express*, 6 March 1909.
37. *Midland Counties Express*, 6 March 1909. Also *Staffordshire Advertiser*, 6 March 1909.
38. *Midland Counties Express*, 6 March 1909.
39. *Midland Counties Express*, 6 March 1909.
40. It is Theresa's account, it should be stressed, which provides the basis of what follows.
41. *Midland Counties Express*, 6 March 1909. See also *Times Law Reports*, xxv, 1909, p. 374.
42. *Midland Counties Express*, 6 March 1909.
43. *Midland Counties Express*, 6 March 1909, T. Harriman.
44. *Express and Star*, 22 March 2006, 1 January 2007.
45. WA, D-NAJ/A/7/3, Nock & Joseland, E. Lawrence to J. Evans, 23 September 1908
46. Nock & Joseland, E. Lawrence to Nock & Joseland, 31 October 1908.
47. Report as to Prisoner's antecedents, R.J.A. Boulton deposition.
48. *Midland Counties Express*, 6 March 1909.
49. *Midland Counties Express*, 6 March 1909, S.A. Carter, A. Spilsbury.
50. Reference mislaid.
51. Davidoff, *et al.*, *The Family Story*, p. 170. See also E. Roberts, *Women's Work, 1840-1940* (Cambridge University Press, 1988), pp. 19-22
52. Davidoff, *et al.*, *The Family Story*, p. 171.
53. J. Benson, *Affluence and Authority: A Social History of Twentieth-Century Britain* (Arnold, 2005), pp. 152-3.

54. *Midland Counties Express*, 6 March 1909; Copy/ police report as to prisoner's antecedents, E. Wardle deposition.
55. It is obviously possible that her account was coloured by a concern to protect the reputation of her dead sister.
56. Copy/Police Report as to prisoner's antecedents, K. Lewis disposition.
57. *Midland Counties Express*, 6 March 1909, R. James, E. Lawrence.

Notes to Chapter 8: 'I have shot a woman'

1. NA, A5516/44/4, 214971, Copy/Police Report as to prisoner's antecedents, T.H. Galbraith deposition.
2. *Express and Star*, 31 December 1908.
3. *Midland Counties Express*, 2 January 1909.
4. *Daily Mail*, 2 January 1909.
5. *Express and Star*, 30 December 1908.
6. Copy/Police Report as to prisoner's antecedents, K. Maddox deposition.
7. A. Brew to *Wolverhampton Chronicle*, 4 June 1999.
8. K. Maddox deposition. Also *Wolverhampton Chronicle*, 13 January 1909; *Midland Counties Express*, 9 January 1909.
9. *Midland Counties Express*, 6 January 1909, A. Finley.
10. K. Maddox deposition; *Midland Counties Express*, 9 January 1909.
11. *Wolverhampton Chronicle*, 13 January 1909; *Midland Counties Express*, 9 January 1909.
12. K. Maddox deposition; *Midland Counties Express*, 9 January 1909.
13. *Wolverhampton Chronicle*, 13 January 1909; *Midland Counties Express*, 9 January 1909.
14. *Wolverhampton Chronicle*, 6 January 1909.
15. K. Maddox deposition; *Midland Counties Express*, 9 January 1909.
16. K. Maddox deposition; *Wolverhampton Chronicle*, 13 January 1909.
17. K. Maddox deposition; *Midland Counties Express*, 9 January 1909.
18. K. Maddox deposition; *Wolverhampton* Chronicle 13 January 1909; *Midland Counties Express*, 9 January 1909.
19. K. Maddox deposition.
20. K. Maddox deposition; *Wolverhampton Chronicle*, 13 January 1909.
21. K. Maddox deposition; *Wolverhampton Chronicle*, 13 January 1909.
22. *Wolverhampton Chronicle*, 13 February 1909; *Midland Counties Express*, 9 January 1909.
23. A.H. Carter deposition.
24. Wolverhampton Register Office, HC 989620, Ruth Hadley death certificate, 29 December 1908.
25. *Wolverhampton Chronicle*, 6 January 1909.
26. Police Report, R.J.A. Bolton deposition.
27. Thomas Hudspeth Galbraith (MB, MS, Aberdeen, 1892). *Court Guide Warwickshire, Worcestershire, and Staffordshire*, 1902, p. 609.
28. T.H. Galbraith deposition.
29. T.H.Galbraith deposition. This account is corroborated, in broad terms, by R.J.A. Boulton deposition.

30. T.H. Galbraith deposition; *Midland Counties Express*, 9 January 1909; *Wolverhampton Chronicle*, 6 January, 13 January 1909.

31. A.H. Carter deposition.

32. *Midland Counties Express*, 9 January 1909.

33. T.H. Galbraith deposition. Cf. *Wolverhampton Chronicle*, 13 January 1909. Also *Midland Counties Express*, 9 January 1909; A.H. Carter deposition.

34. A.H. Carter deposition; T.H. Galbraith deposition; *Midland Counties Express*, 9 January 1909; *Wolverhampton Chronicle*, 13 January 1909. See also G. Haynes deposition.

35. A.H. Carter deposition.

36. T.H. Galbraith deposition; A.H. Carter deposition; *Midland Counties Express*, 9 January 1909; *Wolverhampton Chronicle*, 13 January 1909. Galbraith and Carter compared their notes, and found that 'they agreed'. A.H. Carter deposition.

37. *Wolverhampton Chronicle*, 6 January, 13 January 1909; *Midland Counties Express*, 9 January 1909.

38. A.H. Carter deposition. Also *Midland Counties Express*, 9 January 1909.

39. G. Haynes deposition.

40. G. Haynes deposition; *Express and Star*, 30 December 1908; *Wolverhampton Chronicle*, 6 January 1909; *Wolverhampton Red Book*, 1901, p. 30; *Kelly's Directory of Staffordshire*, 1908, p. 543.

41. D. Woods, 'Community Violence', in J. Benson (ed.), *The Working Class in England 1875–1914* (Croom Helm, 1985), p. 165. Also p. 166; R. Hood and A. Roddam, 'Crime, Sentencing and Punishment', in A.H. Halsey and J. Webb (eds), *Twentieth-Century British Social Trends* (Macmillan, 2000), p. 683.

42. Benson, *Affluence and Authority*, pp. 108–10. See also Woods, 'Community Violence'.

43. F.M.L. Thompson, *The Rise of Respectable Society: A Social History of Victorian Britain, 1830–1900* (Fontana, 1988), p. 330.

44. W. Hill deposition. Also *Staffordshire Advertiser*, 6 March 1909.

45. W. Hill deposition; G. Haynes deposition; *Wolverhampton Chronicle*, 6 January 1909; *Midland Counties Express*, 9 January 1909.

46. *Wolverhampton Chronicle*, 6 January 1909.

47. W. Hill deposition; *Wolverhampton Chronicle*, 6 January, 13 January 1909; *Midland Counties Express*, 9 January 1909.

48. W. Hill deposition.

49. *Midland Counties Express*, 9 January 1909; *WC*, 13 January 1909.

50. G. Haynes deposition. Cf. *Midland Counties Express*, 9 January 1909; *Wolverhampton Chronicle*, 13 January 1909.

51. H. Jones, *Health and Society in Twentieth-Century Britain* (Longman, 1994), pp. 20–1; N. Fox, 'The History of the Royal Hospital': www.localhistory.scit.wlv.ac.uk/articles/Royal Hospital; R. Stallard, *Wolverhampton Hospitals Heritage* (n.p., n.d.), p. 15.

52. A.J. Powell deposition; *Express and Star*, 31 December 1908; *Wolverhampton Chronicle*, 6 January, 13 January 1909; *Midland Counties Express*, 9 January 1909.

Notes to Chapter 9: 'The gravity of his position'

1. NA, A5516/44/4, 214971, Copy/Police Report as to prisoner's antecedents, P.R. Mander to Governor H.M. Prison, Stafford.

2. W. Hill deposition. For the taking of such depositions, see A. Brabin, *The Black Widows of Liverpool: A Chilling Account of Cold-Blooded Murder in Victorian Liverpool* (Palatine Books, 2003), pp. 9–10.

3. W. Hill deposition; *Wolverhampton Chronicle*, 13 January 1909.

4. *Wolverhampton Chronicle*, 13 January 1909.

5. W. Hill deposition; *Wolverhampton Chronicle*, 13 January 1909; *Kelly's Directory of Staffordshire*, 1892, p. 442.

6. W. Hill deposition; *Wolverhampton Chronicle*, 13 January 1909.

7. W. Hill deposition.

8. G. Haynes deposition; *Wolverhampton Chronicle*, 13 January 1909.

9. NA, A5516/44/4, 214971. The file also contains a more grammatical 'copy', and the local press printed a grammatical, but slightly different version. *Wolverhampton Chronicle*, 13 January 1909.

10. *Wolverhampton Chronicle*, 13 January 1909.

11. G. Haynes deposition.

12. Information from Spenser Jones.

13. G. Haynes deposition.

14. Marjoribanks, *Marshall Hall*, p. 269.

15. G. Haynes deposition.

16. G. Haynes deposition.

17. G. Haynes deposition.

18. G. Haynes deposition.

19. K. Maddox deposition.

20. *Midland Counties Express*, 9 January 1909.

21. *Midland Counties Express*, 9 January 1909.

22. A.J. Powell deposition.

23. A.J. Powell deposition.

24. *Express and Star*, 6 January 1909.

25. G. Haynes deposition.

26. *Express and Star*, 30 December 1908, 6 January 1909.

27. *Express and Star*, 6 January 1909.

28. WA, CC/POL/A20, Public Office Book (Police), 1908–9, 30 December 1908; Staffordshire Record Office (SRO), D992/66, Stipendiary Records and Accounts, 30December 1908; *Express and Star*, 6 January 1909.

29. *Midland Counties Express*, 9 January 1909.

30. NA, A5516/44/4, 214971, 'Copy/ Police Report as to prisoner's antecedents'.

31. *Express and Star*, 30 December 1908.

32. *Staffordshire Chronicle*, 9 January 1909; *Kelly's Directory of Staffordshire*, 1912, p. 370; J. Briggs, C. Harrison, A. McInnes and D. Vincent, *Crime and Punishment in England: An Introductory History* (UCL Press, 1996), pp. 230–39. Also P. Priestley, *Victorian Prison Lives* (Methuen, 1985); A. Brown, *English Society and the Prison: Time, Culture and Politics in the Development of the Modern Prison* (Boydell Press, 2003).

33. *Midland Counties Express*, 9 January 1909.

34. J. Sim, *Medical Power in Prisons: The Prison Medical Service in England 1774–1989* (Open University Press, 1990), p. 63.

35. There was a change of governor during the time Edward was in the prison. *Staffordshire Advertiser*, 9 January, 6 February 1909.

36. NA, A5516/44/4, 214971, Copy/ Police Report as to prisoner's antecedents, P.R. Mander to Governor.

37. P.R. Mander to Governor.

38. A.J. Lee, *The Origins of the Popular Press in England 1855–1914* (Croom Helm, 1976), pp. 117–30.

39. *Express and Star*, 30 December 1908.

40. A.M. Bankier deposition.

41. P.R. Mander to Governor.

42. MD, MS (Glasgow, 1885). *Court Guide Warwickshire, Worcestershire, and Staffordshire*, 1902, p. 590.

43. NA, A5516/44/4, 214971, Copy/ Police Report as to prisoner's antecedents, A.M. Bankier deposition. Also *Midland Counties Express*, 9 January 1909.

44. A.M. Bankier deposition, Also *Midland Counties Express*, 9 January 1909.

45. *Express and Star*, 31 December 1908; *Wolverhampton Chronicle*, 6 January 1909.

46. *Express and Star*, 31 December 1908; *Wolverhampton Chronicle*, 6 January 1909.

47. *Express and Star*, 31 December 1908; *Wolverhampton Chronicle*, 6 January 1909. Also *Staffordshire Chronicle*, 2 January 1909.

48. G. Haynes deposition.

49. A.B. Clark deposition.

50. A.B. Clark deposition.

51. G. Haynes deposition.

52. G. Haynes deposition; *Midland Counties Express*, 9 January 1909.

53. G. Haynes deposition.

54. Information from Bill Piggins.

55. For long-term prisoners' perceptions of time, see Brown, *English Society*, ch. 2.

56. *Midland Counties Express*, 9 January 1909.

57. *Midland Counties Express*, 9 January 1909.

58. *Midland Counties Express*, 9 January 1909.

59. *Midland Counties Express*, 9 January 1909.

60. *Midland Counties Express*, 9 January 1909.

61. *Midland Counties Express*, 9 January 1909.

62. *Midland Counties Express*, 9 January 1909.

63. *Midland Counties Express*, 9 January 1909.

64. Interview with Mrs A.

65. *Midland Counties Express*, 9 January 1909.

66. *Midland Counties Express*, 9 January 1909.

67. *Midland Counties Express*, 9 January 1909.

68. *Midland Counties Express*, 9 January 1909.

69. *Midland Counties Express*, 9 January 1909.

70. *Midland Counties Express*, 9 January 1909.

71. *Midland Counties Express*, 9 January 1909.

72. *Midland Counties Express*, 9 January 1909.

73. *Midland Counties Express*, 9 January 1909.

74. *Midland Counties Express*, 9 January 1909.

75. *Midland Counties Express*, 9 January 1909.

76. Police Report as to prisoner's antecedents, deposition cover sheet.

77. *Midland Counties Express*, 9 January 1909.

78. WA, cc/POL/A20, Public Office Book (Police), 1908–9, 8 January 1909; SRO, D992/66, District of South Staffordshire Stipendiary, Records and Accounts, 8 January 1909.
79. *Midland Counties Express*, 9 January 1909.

Notes to Chapter 10: 'A very lucky man'

1. WA, D-NAJ/A/7/3, Nock & Joseland, J. Evans to Mr Nock, 13 March 1909.
2. Information from Bill Piggins.
3. See J. Ogden, 'Trial Gets the Old Bailey Treatment', *Express and Star*, 29 March 1989.
4. *Birmingham Gazette and Express*, 5, 6, 8 March 1909.
5. *Staffordshire Advertiser*, 6, 13 March 1909.
6. *Staffordshire Chronicle*, 6, 13 March 1909.
7. *Express and Star*, 3 March 1909.
8. *Midland Counties Express*, 6, 13 March 1909.
9. *Wolverhampton Chronicle*, 10 March 1909.
10. *Cheshire Daily Echo*, 5 March 1909.
11. *Manchester Guardian*, 8 March 1909.
12. *The Times*, 6, 8 March 1909.
13. B. Roberts, *Murder in the Midlands* (QuercuS: Warwick, 2000), pp. 97–100; 'The Wolverhampton Merchant Accused of Murdering his Mistress – Saved from a Swinging by Britain's Most Brilliant Lawyer', *Black Country Bugle*, 16 September 2004, p. 5.
14. E. Marjoribanks, *The Life of Sir Edward Marshall Hall* (Cedric Chivers, 1929), pp. 266–76.
15. Ogden, 'Old Bailey'.
16. *Express and Star*, 3 March 1909.
17. *Wolverhampton Journal*, February 1907.
18. For Jelf, see also *Express and Star*, 11 November 1907.
19. *Staffordshire Adertiser*, 6 March 1909; *Staffordshire Chronicle*, 6 March 1909.
20. *Wolverhampton Chronicle*, 3 March 1909.
21. *Midland Counties Express*, 6 March 1909.
22. *Staffordshire Advertiser*, 20 February 1909.
23. A.E. Bowker, *Behind the Bar* (Staples Press, 1947), p. 31.
24. A.W. Myers, 'K.C.'s and their Chambers', *Strand Magazine*, 25, 1903, pp. 139–40; Bowker, *Behind the Bar*, pp. 30–31. Also R. Cooper, *Shadow of the Noose* (Penguin, 1989).
25. E. Lustgarten, *Defender's Triumph* (Wingate, n.d.), p. 102. For Marshall Hall's other cases, see for example, F. Bresler, *Scales of Justice* (Weidenfeld & Nicolson, 1973), pp. 10–18, 92–101; R.H. Lewis, *Edwardian Murders* (David & Charles, 1989), ch. 5.
26. Marjoribanks, *Marshall Hall*, Birkenhead's introduction.
27. www.oxford dnb
28. Bowker, *Behind the Bar*, p. 31.
29. Marjoribanks, *Marshall Hall*, p. 269.
30. Bowker, *Behind the Bar*, p. 33,
31. Lustgarten, *Defender's Triumph*, p. 135. Also Marjorianks, *Marshall Hall*, pp. 223–63.

32. *Staffordshire Advertiser*, 13 March 1909. Also *Staffordshire Chronicle*, 13 March 1909.

33. *Staffordshire Advertiser*, 6 March 1909.

34. *Midland Counties Express*, 6 March 1909; Marjoribanks, *Marshall Hall*, p. 269.

35. *Midland Counties Express*, 6 March 1909.

36. *Midland Counties Express*, 6 March 1909.

37. *Midland Counties Express*, 6 March 1909.

38. Marjoribanks, *Marshall Hall*, p. 270.

39. *Midland Counties Express*, 6 March 1909.

40. *Midland Counties Express*, 6 March 1909.

41. *Midland Counties Express*, 6 March 1909; Marjoribanks, *Marshall Hall*, p. 270.

42. *Midland Counties Express*, 6 March 1909.

43. *The Times*, 5 March 1909; *Birmingham Gazette and Express*, 5 March 1909; *Midland Counties Express*, 6 March 1909; *Times Law Reports*, xxv, 1908–9, p. 374.

44. *Birmingham Gazette and* Express, 5 March 1909; *Midland Counties Express*, 6 March 1909.

45. Bowker, *Behind the Bar*, p. 32.

46. For a different, and more dramatic, account, see Bowker, *Behind the Bar*, p. 32.

47. *Midland Counties Express*, 6 March 1909, Marjoribanks, *Marshall Hall*, p. 270.

48. Bowker, *Behind the Bar*, p. 32.

49. Marjoribanks, *Marshall Hall*, p. 270.

50. *Midland Counties Express*, 6 March 1909.

51. Bresler, *Scales of Justice*, p. 98. Also Lustgarten, *Defender's Triumph*, p. 132; Cooper, *Shadow of the Noose*, ch. 19.

52. Marjoribanks, *Marshall Hall*, p. 270.

53. 'The Wolverhampton Merchant', *Black Country Bugle*, 16 September 2004.

54. *Birmingham Gazette and Express*, 5 March 1909; Marjoribanks, *Marshall Hall*, pp. 270–1; Bowker, *Behind the Bar*, p. 33.

55. *Birmingham Gazette and* Express, 5 March 1909; *Midland Counties Express*, 6 March 1909.

56. *Midland Counties Express*, 6 March 1909.

57. *Birmingham Gazette and* Express, 5 March 1909; *Midland Counties Express*, 6 March 1909.

58. *Midland Counties Express*, 6 March 1909.

59. *Midland Counties Express*, 6 March 1909. Also *Birmingham Gazette and Express*, 6 March 1909.

60. *Midland Counties Express*, 6 March 1909.

61. *Midland Counties Express*, 6 March 1909.

62. *Midland Counties Express*, 6 March 1909; *Birmingham Gazette and Express*, 6 March 1909.

63. Marjoribanks, *Marshall Hall*, p. 271.

64. *Midland Counties Express*, 6 March 1909.

65. *Midland Counties Express*, 6 March 1909; *Birmingham Gazette and Express*, 6 March 1909.

66. *Midland Counties Express*, 6 March 1909.

67. Marjoribanks, *Marshall Hall*, pp. 271–2.

68. Marjoribanks, *Marshall Hall*, p. 272. Cf. Lustgarten, *Defender's Triumph*, pp. 136–7.

69. *Birmingham Gazette and Express*, 6 March 1909.

70. See Bowker, *Behind the Bar*, p. 34.
71. *Midland Counties Express*, 6 March 1909.
72. *Midland Counties Express*, 6 March 1909. Also *Birmingham gazette and Express*, 6 March 1909.
73. Marjoribanks, *Marshall Hall*, p. 273. Also Bowker, *Behind the Bar*, p. 35.
74. *Midland Counties Express*, 13 March 1909.
75. *Wolverhampton Chronicle*, 10 March 1909. Also *Midland Counties Express*, 13 March 1909; *Birmingham Gazette and Express*, 8 March 1909. Cf. Marjoribanks, *Marshall Hall*, pp. 273–5.
76. *Staffordshire Advertiser*, 13 March 1909.
77. *Midland Counties Express*, 13 March 1909. Also *Birmingham Gazette and Express*, 8 March 1909.
78. *The Times*, 8 March 1909.
79. *The Times*, 8 March 1909; *Manchester Guardian*, 8 March 1909; *Wolverhampton Chronicle*, 10 March 1909.
80. *The Times*, 8 March 1909. Also *Wolverhampton Chronicle*, 10 March 1909.
81. *Wolverhampton Chronicle*, 10 March 1909.
82. *Staffordshire Advertiser*, 13 March 1909.
83. *Wolverhampton Chronicle*, 10 March 1909.
84. *Express and Star*, 8 March 1909; *Birmingham Gazette and Express*, 8 March 1909; *Wolverhampton Chronicle*, 10 March 1909.
85. Marjoribanks, *Marshall Hall*, p. 276.
86. WA, D-NAJ/A/7/3, Nock & Joseland Papers, J. Evans to Mr Nock, 13 March 1909.

Notes to Chapter 11: 'The nobs all dropped him'

1. Interview with Mrs A.
2. J. Tosh, 'Masculinities in an Industrialising Society: Britain, 1800–1914', *Journal of British Studies*, 44, 2005, p. 331.
3. WA, D-NAJ/A/7/3, Nock and Joseland, J. Evans to Mr Nock, 13 March 1909.
4. Interview with Mrs B.
5. Interview with Mrs A.
6. *Staffordshire Chronicle*, 13 March 1909.
7. Interview with Mrs A.
8. *Kidderminster Times*, 3 December 1910.
9. E. Marjoribanks, *The Life of Sir Edward Marshall Hall* (Cedric Chivers, 1929), p. 276; B. Roberts, *Murder in the Midlands* (QuercuS: Warwick, 2000), p. 100.
10. SRO, D992/67, Stipendiary District of South Staffordshire, Records and Accounts, 24 March 1909.
11. *Midland Evening News*, 8 December 1909.
12. Nock and Joseland, E. Lawrence to Messrs Nock and Joseland, 14 October 1909. Also letter to Mr Nock, 31 January 1910.
13. *West Bromwich Weekly News*, 17 July 1909.
14. *Wolverhampton Red Book*, 1901, p. 75; *The Wulfrunian*, April 1908, p. 117; *Wolverhampton Grammar School Register 1515–1920* (Titus Wilson, 1926?), pp. 200, 346.
15. *London Gazette*, 12 October 1909.

16. P. Di Martino, 'Approaching Disaster: Personal Bankruptcy Legislation in Italy and England, c. 1880–1939', *Business History*, 47, 2005, p. 36. Also G.R. Rubin and D. Sugarman, *Law, Economy and Society, 1750–1914: Essays in the History of English Law* (Professional Books, 1984), p. 244.

17. See also A. Rodger, 'The Codification of Commercial Law in Victorian Britain', *Law Quartery Review*, 108, 1992.

18. *London Gazette*, 12 October 1909; Nock & Joseland, press cuttings.

19. *Midland Evening News*, 8 December 1909. It was difficult to keep such revelations quiet: see Nock and Joseland, Charles Joseland to Mr Nock, 24 December 1909.

20. Cf. H. Perkin, *The Rise of Professional Society: England since 1880* (Routledge, 1989), p. 92.

21. *Express and Star*, 29 April 1910.

22. *Kidderminster Times*, 16 April 1910.

23. *Kidderminster Times*, 16 April 1910.

24. *Kidderminster Times*, 18 June 1910. See G. Frost, '"She is But a Woman": Kitty Byron and the English Edwardian Criminal Justice System', *Gender & History*, 16, 2004, p. 548.

25. *West Bromwich Weekly News*, 18 June 1910. Also *Kidderminster News*, 16 June 1910; *Kidderminster Times*, 18 June 1910.

26. Nock and Joseland, C. Joseland to J. Nock, 24 December 1909; *Kidderminster Times*, 7 August 1909, 19 February 1910; *Kelly's Directory of Worcestershire*, 1912, pp. 145–51.

27. *Kidderminster News*, 1 December 1910.

28. *Kidderminster Shuttle*, 21 January 1911.

29. *Kidderminster News*, 24 February, 10 March 1910.

30. *Kidderminster Times*, 19 March 1910.

31. *Kidderminster Times*, 19, 26 February 1910.

32. *Kidderminster Times*, 26 March 1910. Also *Kidderminster News*, 31 March 1910.

33. *Kidderminster Shuttle*, 25 February 1911.

34. *Kidderminster News*, 25 August 1910. Also *Kidderminster Times*, 27 August 1910.

35. *Express and Star*, 29 April 1910; *Kidderminster Shuttle*, 28 January 1911.

36. *Kidderminster Shuttle*, 28 January 1911.

37. *Kelly's Directory of Staffordshire*, 1896, p. 592.

38. *Kidderminster Shuttle*, 28 January 1911.

39. *Kidderminster Shuttle*, 28 January 1911.

40. *Kidderminster Shuttle*, 25 February 1911.

41. *Kidderminster Shuttle*, 25 March 1911.

42. *Kidderminster Times*, 25 March 1911.

43. *Kidderminster Shuttle*, 3 September 1908.

44. *Kidderminster Shuttle*, 3 September 1910. Also *Kidderminster Times*, 3 September 1910.

45. *Kidderminster News*, 20 October 1910. Also *Kidderminster Times*, 29 October 1910.

46. *Kidderminster Times*, 15 October 1910; *Kidderminster Shuttle*, 15 October 1910.

47. *Kidderminster Times*, 15 October 1910.

48. *Kidderminster Shuttle*, 15 October 1910.

49. *Kidderminster Times*, 15 October 1910.

50. *Kidderminster Times*, 15 April 1911.

Notes to Chapter 12: 'I've plenty of money'

1. *Kidderminster Shuttle*, 28 January 1911.
2. *Kidderminster News*, 17 March 1910.
3. P. Johnson, 'Class Law in Victorian England', *Past and Present*, 141, 1993.
4. *Kidderminster Times*, 26 March 1910.
5. *Kidderminster Times*, 26 March 1910; *Kidderminster Shuttle*, 25 February 1911.
6. *Kidderminster Times*, 7 August 1909; *Kidderminster Shuttle*, 25 February 1911, 21 September 1912.
7. Advertisement in *Kidderminster Shuttle*, 10 June 1911.
8. He was living in 'The Lea' by the end of 1909. See WA, D-NAJ/A/7/3, Nock & Joseland, C. Joseland to J Nock, 24 December 1909; *Kidderminster Times*, 19 February 1910.
9. *Express and Star*, 29 April 1910; *Kidderminster Shuttle*, 28 January 1911. He also hired other tradesmen. *Kidderminster Times*, 15 October 1910.
10. *Kidderminster Times*, 15 October 1910.
11. *Kidderminster Shuttle*, 21, 28 September 1912.
12. S. Gunn and R. Bell, *Middle Classes: Their Rise and Sprawl* (Cassell, 2002), p. 38.
13. *Kidderminster News*, 20 October 1910; *Kidderminster Times*, 29 October 1910.
14. *Kidderminster News*, 25 August 1910. Also *Kidderminster Shuttle*, 27 August 1910.
15. *Kidderminster Shuttle*, 15 October 1910.
16. Eleanor Beaton had probably worked for him for some time because when he drew up his will in May 1912, he left her the sum of £25 (on condition that she was still in his service at the time of his death). *Kidderminster Times*, 15 April 1910; Probate Registry, York, 05/01/0296, Edward Lawrence will, 27 May 1912.
17. *Kidderminster Shuttle*, 3 September 1910; Kidderminster *News*, 25 August 1910; *Kidderminster Times*, 27 August, 29 October, 3 December 1910.
18. *Kidderminster Times*, 3 September 1910, 15 April 1911.
19. *Kidderminster Shuttle*, 29 October 1910; *Kidderminster Times*, 25 March 1911. Cock-fighting was a 'sport' which had been outlawed as early as 1849. See J. Pinfold, 'Dandy Rats at Play: The Liverpudlian Middle Classes and Horse-Racing in the Nineteenth Century', in M. Huggins and J.A. Mangan (eds), *Disreputable Pleasures: Less Virtuous Victorians at Play* (Cass, 2004).
20. *Kidderminster Times*, 25 March 1911.
21. *Kidderminster Times*, 16 April, 18 June 1910.
22. *Kidderminster Times*, 16 April 1910.
23. *Kidderminster Times*, 16 April 1910.
24. *Kidderminster Shuttle*, 3 September 1910.
25. *Kidderminster News*, 20 October 1910.
26. *Kidderminster News*, 17 March 1910.
27. *Kidderminster News*, 25 August 1910.
28. *Kidderminster News*, 17 March 1910.
29. *Kidderminster News*, 25 August 1910.
30. *Kidderminster Times*, 26 February 1910.
31. *Kidderminster Times*, 18 June, 3 December 1910
32. A.E. Bowker, *Behind the Bar* (Staples Press, 1947), p. 29.
33. Probate Registry, York, 05/01/0296, E. Lawrence probate, 21 September 1912.

34. W.D. Rubinstein, *Men of Property: The Very Wealthy in Britain since the Industrial Revolution* (Croom Helm, 1981); W.D. Rubinstein, 'The Victorian Middle Classes: Wealth, Occupation, and Geography', *Economic History Review*, xxx, 1977.
35. *Kidderminster Times*, 25 August 1910.
36. For example, *Kidderminster Times*, 24 February 1910; 15 April 1911.
37. *Kidderminster Times*, 15 October 1910.
38. *Kidderminster News*, 25 August 1910.
39. *Midland Counties Express*, 10 August 1912.
40. *Midland Counties Express*, 17 August 1912; *Who Was Who 1897–1915* (Black, 1966?), p. 199.

Notes to Chapter 13: Gender, class and respectability

1. *Express and Star*, 9 August 1912; *Midland Counties Express*, 10 August 1912.
2. B. Franklin and D. Murphy, *What's News? The Market, Politics and the Local Press* (Routledge, 1991), p. 2. Also B. Franklin and D. Murphy, *Making the Local News* (Routledge, 1998).
3. However, it is said within the Lawrence family that Edward admitted subsequently that his killing of Ruth had been deliberate. Information from Tim Sheldon.
4. A. J. Hammerton, *Cruelty and Companionship: Conflict in Nineteenth-Century Married Life* (Routledge, 1992), p. 169.
5. For working-class respectability as 'a role rather than as an ideology or a uniform life-style', see P. Bailey, *Leisure and Class in Victorian England: Rational Recreation and the Contest For Control, 1830–1885* (Methuen, 1987), pp. 184–5. Also P. Bailey, '"Will the Real Bill Banks Stand Up?": A Role Analysis of Mid-Victorian Working-Class Respectability', *Journal of Social History*, xii, 1979. See too S.O. Rose, *Limited Livelihoods: Gender and Class in Nineteenth-Century England* (University of California Press, 1992), ch.6.
6. M. Huggins and J.A. Mangan, 'Prologue: All Mere Compexities', in M. Huggins and J.A. Mangan (eds), *Disreputable Pleasures: Less Virtuous Victorians at Play* (Cass, 2004), p. xx.
7. S. Gunn and R. Bell, *Middle Classes: Their Rise and Sprawl* (Cassell, 2002), p. 93. Also p. 94.
8. M. Huggins, 'Cartoons and Comic Periodicals, 1841–1901: A Satirical Sociology of Victorian Sporting Life', in Huggins and Mangan (eds), *Disreputable Pleasures*, pp. 129–30, 143
9. See J. Foster, *Men-at-the Bar: A Biographical Handlist* (Hazell, Watson and Viney, 1885), p. 434; *Who's Who*, 1913, p. 1866.
10. *Kidderminster Times*, 18 June 1910.
11. *West Bromwich Weekly News*, 29 October 1910.
12. *Wolverhampton Chronicle*, 10 March 1909.
13. *Wolverhampton Chronicle*, 10 March 1909.
14. WA, D-NAJ/A/7/3, Nock & Joseland papers, J. Evans to Mr Nock, 13 March 1909.
15. *Midland Counties Express*, 10 August 1912.
16. NA, A5516/44/4, 214971, Copy/Police Report as to prisoner's antecedents, L.R. Burnett to Director of Public Prosecutions, 29 January 1908 [1909].
17. L.R. Burnett to Director of Public Prosecutions, 29 January 1908 [1909].

Select bibliography

Manuscript sources

National Archives
Copy/Police Report as to Prisoner's Antecedents
High Court of Justice, Probate, Divorce and Admiralty Division, Lawrence *v.* Lawrence

Probate Registry, York
Probate Records

Royal College of Veterinary Surgeons
Dead Members' File

Staffordshire Record Office
District of South Staffordshire Stipendary, Records and Accounts

Union Grand Lodge of England
Lodge Bye-Laws
Membership Registers
Lists of Contributing Members

Wolverhampton Archives
Alehouses, Register of Licences
Borough of Wolverhampton Record Books
Nock & Joseland Papers

Wolverhampton Register Office
Birth, Death and Marriage Certificates

Official publications

Census of England and Wales

Directories

Court Guide Warwickshire, Worcestershire and Staffordshire
Hulley's Hardware District Directory
Kelly's Directory of Staffordshire
Kelly's Directory of Warwickshire
Porter's Directory of Salop
Post Office Directory of Bath
Slater's Directory of Edinburgh and Leith
White's Directory of Birmingham

Newspapers and periodicals

Bath Herald
Birmingham Gazette and Express
Express and Star
Kidderminster News
Kidderminster Shuttle
Kidderminster Times
Licensed Victuallers' Gazette
Midland Counties Express
Midland Evening News
Newport and Market Drayton Advertiser
Scottish Leader
Staffordshire Advertiser
Veterinary Record
Wellington Standard
West Bromwich Weekly News
Wolverhampton Chronicle

Books and articles

Burt, R., 'Freemasonry and Business Networking during the Victorian Period', *Economic History Review*, lvi, 2003

Davidoff, L., 'Class and Gender in Victorian England: The Case of Hannah Cullwick and A.J. Munby', *Feminist Studies*, 5, 1979

Davidoff, L., *Worlds Between: Historical Perspectives on Gender and Class* (Polity Press, 1995)

Davidoff, L., Fink, J. and Holden, K., *The Family Story: Blood, Contract and Intimacy 1830–1960* (Longman, 1999)

Fisher, J.R., 'Not Quite a Profession: The Aspirations of Veterinary Surgeons in England in the mid Nineteenth Century', *Historical Research*, 66, 1993

Frost, G., '"She is but a Woman": Kitty Byron and the English Edwardian Criminal Justice System', *Gender & History*, 16, 2004

Gillis, J.R., *For Better, For Worse: British Marriages 1600 to the Present* (Oxford University Press, 1985)

Gunn, S. and Bell, R., *Middle Classes: Their Rise and Sprawl* (Cassell, 2002)

Hall, C., *White, Male and Middle Class: Explorations in Feminism and History* (Polity Press, 1992)

Hammerton, A.J., *Cruelty and Companionship: Conflict in Nineteenth-Century Married Life* (Routledge, 1992)

Huggins, M. (ed.), *Disreputable Pleasures: Less Virtuous Victorians at Play* (Cass, 2004)

Huggins, M.J., 'More Sinful Pleasures? Leisure, Respectability and the Male Middle Classes in Victorian England', *Journal of Social History*, Spring 2000

Johnson, P., 'Class Law in Victorian England', *Past and Present*, 141, 1993

Lawrence, J., 'Class and Gender in the Making of Urban Toryism, 1880–1914', *English Historical Review*, 108, 1993

McLaren, A., *The Trials of Masculinity: Policing Sexual Boundaries, 1870–1930* (University of Chicago Press, 1997)

Marjoribanks, E., *The Life of Sir Edward Marshall Hall* (Gollancz, 1929)

Roper, M. and Tosh, J. (eds), *Manful Assertions: Masculinities in Britain since 1800* (Routledge, 1991).

Tosh, J., 'What Should Historians do with Masculinity? Reflections on Nineteenth-Century Britain', *History Workshop Journal*, 38, 1994

Tosh, J., 'Gentlemanly Politeness and Manly Simplicity in Victorian England', *Transactions of the Royal Historical Society*, 12, 2002

Thompson, F.M.L., *The Rise of Respectable Society: A Social History of Victorian Britain 1830–1900* (Fontana, 1988)

Trainor, R.H., *Black Country Elites: The Exercise of Authority in an Industrialized Area 1830–1900* (Clarendon Press, 1993)

Wiener, M.J., 'The Sad Story of George Hall: Adultery, Murder and the Politics of Mercy in Mid-Victorian England', *Social History*, 24, 1999